Explosion of a Memory

Explosion of a Memory

WRITINGS BY

Heiner Müller

✠—✠—✠—✠—✠—✠—✠—✠

Edited and Translated by Carl Weber

PAJ PUBLICATIONS
NEW YORK

For Marianne

© 1989 Copyright by PAJ Publications
© 1989 Copyright of texts in the original held by Verlag der Autoren, Frankfurt, West Germany, representing Henschel Verlag, Berlin/DDR.
© 1989 Translation, preface, and introductory materials copyright by Carl Weber.

Library of Congress Cataloging in Publication Data
Explosion of a Memory
Library of Congress Catalog Card No.: 88-62673
ISBN: 1-55554-040-6 (cloth)
ISBN: 1-55554-041-4 (paper)

Printed in the United States of America

Publication of this book has been made possible in part by grants received from the National Endowment for the Arts, Washington, D.C., a federal agency, and the New York State Council on the Arts.

The translation of *Explosion of a Memory* was made possible, in part, by a grant from The Wheatland Foundation.

Contents

WRITING FACE TO FACE WITH HISTORY

Carl Weber

When HAMLETMACHINE *and Other Texts for the Stage,* a first collection in English of plays by Heiner Müller, was published in 1984, the author was practically unknown in the United States. Since then several of his plays have been widely performed. Müller's collaboration with the director Robert Wilson, who created productions based on texts by Müller in Cambridge, Massachusetts, and New York, has received considerable attention and acclaim. In Europe, his importance for contemporary letters and the theatre is generally acknowledged by now. He is the rare writer who has been awarded the most prestigious literary prizes of both Germanies: the Mülheim and the Büchner Prize of the Federal Republic, and the National Prize of the GDR; a ''Werkschau'' and conference on Müller's work in Berlin, 1988, assembled theatre workers and scholars from many countries to view productions of his plays and discuss his writings.

In 1984, the volume HAMLETMACHINE presented all the stage texts Müller had written since his first visit to America in 1975, with the addition of an early work, THE CORRECTION. This second selection contains all of Müller's writings for performance since 1984, and a sampling of other recent texts. It also offers two earlier works: a collection of poetry and narrative prose, A B C, most of it written in the early fifties yet already anticipating many of the themes and issues that reappear through Müller's work, as will become evident in the other earlier text, GERMANIA DEATH IN BERLIN. This play, which Müller worked on from 1956 to 1971, represents a turning point in his work, being his first effort at a genre he later elected to name "synthetic fragment." It also marks the transition from texts that focused foremost on the struggle of building Socialism in his country, the GDR, to writing that delves into the dark past of German history to explore what one might call the "collective unconscious" of his nation.

* * *

The distance covered in this volume lies not merely in the thirty-eight years which have passed since Müller sketched the first texts of ABC. These writings reflect an author's long and controversial passage through history with results that are indeed unusual in contemporary theatre and literature. Müller began writing poetry and narrative that recorded not only his responses to German Fascism and the Socialism established in East Germany after World War II, but to personal tragedy as well. He then moved on to his "synthetic fragments"—wildly imaginative and as satiric as they were painfully serious—which are represented by GERMANIA DEATH IN BERLIN, and several texts published in HAMLETMACHINE, to arrive at that one, seemingly never-ending, sentence of EXPLOSION OF A MEMORY, the latter partly created by an act of "automatic writing" as it once was postulated by the Surrealists. Finally, Müller returned to the "Lehrstück," a model he had explored so thoroughly during the sixties but which he refunctioned and reshaped now in his most recent work, VOLOKOLAMSK HIGHWAY.

Other selected writings—speeches, a letter to Robert Wilson, and the concluding interview—trace Müller's recent development and his sometimes unsettling turnabouts. These texts also show him as a writer of multiple perspectives and astounding skills.

* * *

In a 1986 interview for *Performing Arts Journal* Müller stated: "I'm never interested in technique. I never had technical problems and so I'm not interested in discussions about [them] . . . It's just that you have it and you use it . . . The more you write the more you begin to be silent about writing.'' In other words, his experience was that language, whatever it may be defined as in structure or spirit, is a most malleable material, something he always could shape at will. This experience and the gifts that were nurturing it are evident in the texts published here. The bold use he made of his skills caused trouble more often than not for Müller. He was reprimanded for aesthetic and political reasons by critics as well as politicians, not to mention other confrontations his always independent stance has provoked.

* * *

Brecht has often been named as one of Müller's literary ''fathers,'' and his emulation of Brecht's models as well as his later revolt against them both offer ample proof of such parentage. Another ''father'' he once paid reverence to in a short haiku-like poem is Georg Büchner, and Müller's synthetic fragments clearly show that he owes a debt to the author of *Woyzeck* and *Danton's Death*. The third of his ''fathers'' to whom he dedicated a poem (all three poems appear in the HAMLETMACHINE volume) was Vladimir Mayakovsky, whose influence has been more instrumental than most Western readers may recognize. The free-wheeling use of idiom Mayakovsky was so effective in and famous for, his daring appropriation of language and reckless disdain for its rules, all done in the name of revolutionary mission and poetic vigor, was something Müller adopted with all of his heart.

Mayakovsky once stated about his own writing: ''Our usual punctuation, with full stops, commas, etc., is far too poor and limited in expression in comparison with those shades of emotions which the complex man of today compresses into his poetic productions.'' That sentence reads like a comment on several texts in this volume. Indeed, it could have been written by Müller himself, though he probably wouldn't have limited his statement to ''shades of emotion'' only.

* * *

Since the early seventies, when Müller broke with the tradition of linear fable, of consistency in structure and language as well as with other dramaturgic conventions, be they of Aristotle's or Brecht's making, each of his new texts surprised, even shocked, admirers and detractors alike. Whenever one thought to have pegged his style or his ideological position, the next play established a different style and/or changed a philosophical perspective. He often claimed that "to use Brecht without criticizing him amounts to treason," and he truly adopted such an attitude towards his own work where many a new text represented an implicit critique of previous positions. However, the principle of distanciation, of estranging the content and form of a text, has become the one stable element in his work where nearly every new play breaks with whatever conventions the preceding one appeared to have established. Confounding all expectations his audience may have derived from past experience of his work, he defamiliarizes the new piece and enforces a fresh, as yet unconditioned way of reading it or viewing it. There is hardly another contemporary author and surely no dramatist who has changed, so often and so drastically, the poetic and dramaturgic paradigms in his work as Müller.

*   *   *

Throughout these transformations, however, certain themes and subjects can be traced in all his writings. Georg Wieghaus chose two of them for the title of his excellent, exhaustive book on Müller's aesthetics and politics, *Between Task and Treason* (*Zwischen Auftrag und Verrat*, Frankfurt, 1984). Both themes are easily discovered in the selected texts. The often fatal contradiction between an accepted task or mission of a social, usually revolutionary, kind and the committed individual's desire or claim to achieve personal, often sensual, fulfillment in life are at the center of much of Müller's work. Among other themes he has dealt with again and again are: utopia versus despair; idealistic or romantic notions of humanity's progress shattered by the brutal realities of our "prehistory," as Müller calls all human history till the present. Or: ideology shrouding the primeval urge of violence, remnant of mankind's barbarian past.

Early in his writing Müller worked towards a solution, a synthesis of such antithetic positions. Since the early seventies he has taken an increasingly ambiguous stance: he poses the contradictions without resolving them or offers answers which are but provisional solutions. In each case, readers/spectators are challenged to arrive at their own conclusions. This will often invite them to embrace the "impurity" of conflicting positions and also to accept the impurities of any viable solution.

Müller's long march through more than fifty years of history

—and he continuously participated in its struggles while writing about them—has led him from a realm of clear ideological choices into territory where not much seems very sure any longer. Here the collective memory of Western culture is as much poisoning as it is nourishing the ground that spawns all present choices; here Walter Benjamin's Angel of History is buried under an avalanche of rocks. As Müller once described it, the angel's wings move ever more weakly until they may come to a halt.

Müller has often claimed that an author of our age needs to look "into the white of history's eye." He has learned not to flinch anymore at what he sees there. One honorable choice remains, as he concludes in the interview at the end of this collection: To keep writing as long as it's possible—without hope and without despair.

* * *

I'd like to thank Dr. Karlheinz Braun of Verlag der Autoren, Frankfurt, for his support and encouragement of this project, and Bonnie Marranca and Gautam Dasgupta of PAJ Publications for their firm belief in Heiner Müller's work and their help in putting together this book.

A B C

A B C is a collection of texts of which most were written during the early fifties. THE FATHER was written in 1958; ALONE WITH THESE BODIES, YESTERDAY ON A SUNNY AFTERNOON, and OBITUARY in 1975-76. THE IRON CROSS was first published in *Neue Deutsche Literatur*, Berlin, 1/1956; PHILOCTETES 1950 in a volume of GDR poetry, *In Diessem Besseren Land*, Halle, 1966; THE FATHER in *Wespennest*, Vienna, 25/1977; ALONE WITH THESE BODIES in the volume *Theaterbuch 1*, Munich, 1975; OBITUARY, then titled ''Deserts of Love,'' in *Literaturmagazin #4*, Reinbek, 1975. The author arranged these texts with previously unpublished poems, prose, and one playlet in their present configuration for the collected texts edition by Rotbuch Verlag, Berlin; they were published in this order in *Rotbuch #176, Germania Tod In Berlin*, 1977.

The texts in their carefully composed sequence can be read in many ways; for instance, as a free rendering of Heiner Müller's personal story from 1933 to 1976, telling of, or interpreting, incisive historical events and personal experiences as well as reflecting the author's spontaneous or studied responses during those troubled years.

They also might be viewed as a ''catalogue of gestures,'' and they present most of the issues which have been recurrent themes in Müller's writings up to the present. Some of the prose pieces later became stage texts: THE IRON CROSS appeared as Scene 3 of THE BATTLE; SCHOTTERBECK became the scene THE BROTHERS 2 in GERMANIA; the text beginning ''The peasants stood with their backs . . .'' contains the core of the play MAUSER. Various themes of THE FATHER, or of OBITUARY, surface again and again in later writings, and pervading all of these texts are the two topics of Treason and Violence, both of them—more often than not—fatal. They are central to Müller's work, as is the topic of patricide—and its opposite—which both appear in A B C, and in his later work.

The texts then offer occasion to compare and study Müller's

casting of his themes and fables in different forms. One discovers that experimentation with structure and genre isn't done so much to arrive at the most fitting form for a given content—a rather traditional approach—but to capture several of the many angles by which the content may be viewed, and thus invite the ever new, multiple insights such revisioning provides.

Most of the texts reflect German history, from the Thirty Years War (Grobianus) to the "Real Socialism" of today's German Democratic Republic, and many deal with very personal traumas. The brief paragraph "The peasants stood with their backs . . ." refers to the Russian Post-Revolutionary Civil War in 1919-1920; whereas the poem A HUNDRED STEPS retells an episode from Daniel Defoe's *A Journal of the Plague Year*. SCHOTTERBECK describes an event in an East German prison during the uprising of June 17, 1953. PHILOCTETES 1950 is, of course, a rendering of Homer's tale; later Müller wrote a play and also a ballet scenario based on the same story. THE VOYAGE is the only adaptation from the Japanese Noh theatre Müller has published; it is revealing that he studied this ancient Asian tradition at a time when he was trying to evolve his own variant of the didactic play, following the example of Brecht who had become fascinated by the Japanese form twenty years earlier.

In its entirety, A B C appears as a carefully constructed "synthetic" fragment, an example of the literary form Müller began to develop in the seventies. One could argue that A B C is even closer to such a concept than Müller's theatre texts from those years, be it GERMANIA DEATH IN BERLIN; GUNDLINGS LIFE FREDERICK OF PRUSSIA LESSING'S SLEEP DREAM SCREAM or HAMLETMACHINE.

C. W.

DON'T LAUGH BUT IF A TOWN HAS PERISHED
(Grobianus)
I WANT TO BE A GERMAN
(Entry in the exercise book of an eleven-year-old Jewish boy in
the Warsaw Ghetto)
THE TERROR OF WHICH I WRITE ISN'T FROM GERMANY
IT IS A TERROR OF THE SOUL
(Edgar Allan Poe)
THE TERROR I WRITE OF IS FROM GERMANY

AND BETWEEN ABC AND TWO TIMES TWO
We pissed whistling at the school house wall
The teacher whispered through his teeth
DON'T YOU FEEL ANY SHAME We didn't.

When night did fall we climbed the tree
From which at dawn the dead was cut. Empty
Stood his tree now. We said: THAT WAS ONE MAN.
WHERE ARE THE OTHERS? BETWEEN BRANCH AND
  GROUND IS SPACE.

THE IRON CROSS

In April 1945, a stationer at Stargard in Mecklenburg decided to shoot his wife, his fourteen-year-old daughter, and himself. He had heard from customers about Hitler's wedding and suicide.

A reserve corps officer in World War One, he still owned a revolver, and two rounds of ammunition.

When his wife brought in the dinner from the kitchen, he stood at the table and cleaned his gun. He had pinned the Iron Cross to his lapel, as he usually did only on national holidays.

The Führer had chosen suicide, he stated in reply to her question, and he'd be loyal to him, if she, his wedded wife, would be ready to follow him in this, too. He wouldn't doubt that his daughter preferred an honorable death from her father's hand to a life without honor.

He called her. She didn't disappoint him.

Without waiting for his wife's answer, he asked both to put on their coats, since he was going to lead them to a suitable place outside of town to avoid drawing any attention. They obeyed. He then loaded the revolver, had the daughter help him into his coat, locked the apartment, and threw the key through the slit of the mailbox.

It was raining as they walked through the blacked-out streets and out of town, the man in front, without ever looking back at the women who followed at some distance. He heard their steps on the pavement.

After he had left the road and taken the path to the beech grove, he turned to them and urged them to hurry. Because of the night wind that blew with increasing force across the treeless plain, their steps made no noise on the rain drenched ground.

He yelled to them that they should walk ahead. Following them, he didn't know: was he afraid they could run away or did he himself wish to run. It didn't take long and they were far ahead. When he couldn't see them any longer, he realized that he was much too afraid to simply run away and he very much wished they would do so. He stopped and passed his water. He carried the revolver in the pocket of his pants, he felt it cold through the thin fabric. As he walked faster to catch up with the women, the weapon bumped against his leg with each step. He walked more slowly. But when he reached into the pocket to throw the revolver away, he saw his wife and daughter. They stood in the middle of the path and waited for him.

He had intended to do it in the grove but the danger that the shots would be heard wasn't any greater here. When he took the revolver in his hand and released the safety catch, the wife embraced him, sobbing. She was heavy and he had difficulty in shaking her off. He stepped up to the daughter who stared at him, pressed the revolver against her temple and pulled the trigger with his eyes closed. He had hoped the gun wouldn't fire but he heard the shot and saw how the girl reeled and fell.

The wife trembled and screamed. He had to hold her. Only after the third shot was she still.

He was alone.

There was no one who ordered him to put the revolver's muzzle against his own temple. The dead didn't see him, no one saw him.

He pocketed the revolver and bent down to his daughter. Then he began to run.

He ran all the way back to the road and then down the road, though not in the direction of the town but westward. Then he sat down at the roadside, his back against a tree, and considered his situation, breathing heavily. He discovered there was some hope.

He had only to keep running, always to the west, and avoid the nearest villages. Somewhere he could then disappear, more so in a larger city, under another name, an unknown refugee, ordinary and hard-working.

He threw the revolver in the roadside ditch and got up. As he was walking he remembered that he had forgotten to throw away the Iron Cross. He did.

The peasants stood with their backs to the quarry. He looked at the peasants, the peasants looked at him. Their eyes were wide with fear, then narrow with hate, then wide again, then narrow again. He looked at their hands: they were worn-out, then at his own worn-out hand that was sweating. He said the often said phrase louder than usual: FIRE AT THE ENEMIES OF THE REVOLUTION and he fired first. The volley scattered the three bodies down the grassy slope into the quarry.

A HUNDRED STEPS
(After Defoe)

In the century of the Plague
A man lived in Bow, north of London
A boatman, without means or distinction, but
Loyal to his family. Prudent too
In his loyalty.
From the town's downriver
Where the Plague was
He hauled food upriver
To the well-to-do, fearful
On their ships
Midstream.
Thus the pestilence nourished him.
But in the hut
With his wife and the four-year-old
The Plague was too.
And every night he hauled a sack with provisions
Fruit of a day's work, up from the river to a stone
                a hundred steps away from the hut.
Then, retreating, he called the wife. Watching
How she picked up the sack, observing attentively each
                of her movements
He stood for a while
In the safe distance
And returned her salutation.

SCHOTTERBECK when he, on a June morning in 1953, collapsed with a sigh of relief under the blows of those who were in prison with him, heard in the noise of the approaching tanks outside, muffled by the thick Prussian walls of his prison, the tune of the International, never to be forgotten.

PHILOCTETES 1950

Philoctetes, in his hands the bow of Heracles,
       sick with
Leprosy, on Lemnos island, empty without him,
       marooned
By the princes with little provisions, he didn't
       show any
Pride but screamed till the boat disappeared, not held by
       his scream.
And got accustomed, the island's ruler but also
       its slave
Chained to it with the chains of the waters around it,
       of herbage
He lived and of game, sufficient to him for more than
       nine years.
But in the tenth ineffectual year of the war
       the princes
Remembered who they abandoned. How he handled the bow,
       from afar
Deadly. And boats they sent forth that should carry home
       the hero
That he'd adorn them with glory. But he showed himself then
       from his
Proudest side. With violence they had to drag him onto
       the boat
To satisfy his pride. Thus he made up for
       his loss.

THE VOYAGE
(After Motekiyo)

Kagekiyo. Hitomaru. A Woodcutter. Chorus.

1

HITOMARU: Kagekiyo went to battle for Heike. Heike sent him into exile after the battle. He lives in Myazaki. I am not used to travel but I want to go to him. He is my father.
He is old.
(*Sings.*)
The voyage
Is hard.
I pass through the province of Sagami.
Totomi I leave behind me.
I cross the bay in a narrow rented boat.
When will I be in Myazaki?

2

KAGEKIYO: Here in Myazaki I spend my life, under the thatched roof. I, Kagekiyo, the exile who went to battle for Heike. Blind, not knowing the passing of time. My property: one coat for summer and winter. My body: a bundle of bones.
CHORUS:
See the feared one
See the bundle of bones!
His sword is broken.
His sword
Has broken him.
HITOMARU: Here in Myazaki I will ask for my father. (*To Kagekiyo.*) Where is Kagekiyo living, the exile who went to battle for Heike?
KAGEKIYO: (*Remains silent.*)
HITOMARU: (*Walks on.*)
KAGEKIYO: This woman is my daughter. I loved her mother in Atsuta. I found the child of no use and gave her away.

3

HITOMARU: Where is Kagekiyo living, the exile who went to

battle for Heike?
WOODCUTTER: Under the thatched roof.
HITOMARU: The beggar?
WOODCUTTER: Yes.

4

WOODCUTTER: Hey, Kagekiyo!
KAGEKIYO: I am an old piece of iron, of no use. Who is Kagekiyo?
CHORUS:
   The exile
   Ponders the time when he was famous and bloody.
   The blood is still on his hand.
   Where is his fame?
KAGEKIYO: Wind is coming from the mountain. Snow is coming
   behind the wind. I hear how high tide is assaulting the beach. I
   heard it when I went into battle for Heike and after the battle.
   Who is asking for Kagekiyo?
WOODCUTER: Who are you?
HITOMARU: Hitomaru, daughter of Kagekiyo, who for Heike . . .
WOODCUTTER: Your daughter is asking for you.
KAGEKIYO: I am covered with scurf and shame. She is young.
HITOMARU: The voyage was hard. Rain in Sagami, in Totomi
   snow. Across the bay in a rented boat.
KAGEKIYO: (*Sings.*)
   In the boats of the men from Heike's crew
   Loudly acclaimed above others was Kagekiyo.
   Courageous were his men, fast when sailing.
   Now the leader himself is
   worn out.
WOODCUTTER: (*Sits on the ground, eats.*) Tell her the story.

5

KAGEKIYO: Heike's crew came on boats. The foe stood at the
   shore. He had beaten us in the mountains of Harima. He was
   smart and fast. Kagekiyo went ashore with Heike's men and the
   enemy fell upon them. Kagekiyo drove them before him, friend
   and foe alike. He sang:
      Our general doesn't like the other general's nose.
      But he likes his rice paddies well. Run, you dogs!

WOODCUTTER: (*To Hitomaru.*) They were dogs before him. Now he can't lift a leg anymore.

KAGEKIYO: Kagekiyo brandished the spear. Terrible is your arm, Myonoya screamed. Tough is your neck, Kagekiyo shouted. They laughed after the battle. That was Kagekiyo.

WOODCUTTER: The brandisher of spears.

CHORUS:
The exile has told his story. The daughter
Is silent.
Shall she leave him whom no one helps at the end
of his career?
Shall she stay with him whose cheeks won't be
filled by the blood once shed?

THE FATHER

A dead father would perhaps
Have been a better father. Best
Is a stillborn father.
Always anew grass grows over the border.
The grass must be torn up
Again and again as it grows over the border.

1

In 1933, January 31 at 4 a.m., my father, a functionary of the Social-Democratic Party of Germany, was arrested from his bed. I woke up, the sky outside the window black, noise of voices and footsteps. In the next room, books were thrown to the floor. I heard my father's voice, higher than the other voices. I climbed out of bed and went to the door. Through a crack I saw how a man was hitting my father in the face. Freezing, the cover pulled up to the chin, I lay in bed when the door to my room opened. My father stood in the door, behind him the strangers, big, in brown uniforms. There were three of them. One held the door open with his hand. The light was in my father's back, I couldn't see his face. I heard him softly call my name. I didn't answer and lay very still. Then my father said: He's asleep. The door was closed. I heard how they led him away, then the short step of my mother who came back alone.

2

My friends, sons of a low-ranking official, explained to me after my father's arrest that they weren't allowed to play with me anymore. It was on a morning, snow was lying in the roadside ditches, there was a cold wind. I found my friends inside the tool shed in the backyard, sitting on wood blocks. They played with tin soldiers. Outside the door I had heard how they imitated the roar of cannons. When I entered they became silent and looked at each other. Then they continued playing. They placed the tin soldiers in battle arrays facing each other and took turns rolling marbles toward the enemy front. While doing so, they imitated the roar of cannon. They addressed each other as Herr General and called out triumphantly the casualties after each charge. The soldiers died like flies. The war was fought for a pudding. Eventually, one of the generals had no soldiers left, all his army was flat on the floor. This decided the contest. The soldiers killed in action, friend and foe pell mell, were thrown into the cardboard box, along with the one survivor. The generals got up. They would have breakfast now, said the winner and, passing me, he added that I couldn't come along, they weren't allowed to play with me anymore, my father being a criminal. My mother had told me who the criminals were. But also, that it wasn't good to name them. So I didn't tell my friends. They learned twelve years later, sent into the fire by great generals, under the roar of countless real cannons during the terrible last battles of World War II, killing and being killed.

3

One year after my father's arrest, my mother received permission to visit him in the camp. We took a narrow gauge railway to its last station. The road climbed uphill in curves, it passed a sawmill with the smell of freshly cut timber. On the flat top of the mountain the path to the camp branched off. The fields alongside the path were fallow. Then we stood in front of the wide gate with its meshed wire until they brought my father. Looking through the wire mesh, I saw him approaching on the camp road covered with gravel. The closer he came the slower he walked. The convict's garb was too large for him, consequently he looked very small. The gate wasn't opened. He couldn't touch our hands through the narrow wire mesh. I had to step very close to the gate to see his thin face completely. He was very pale. I can't remember what he said. Behind my father stood the armed guard with a round, rosy face.

I wished my father were a shark
Who tore to pieces forty whalers
(And in their blood I'd learned to swim)
My mother a blue whale my name Lautréamont
Died in Paris 1871 unknown

4

Because she was a woman, my mother didn't get work. She accepted the offer of a manufacturer who had been a member of the Social Democratic Party until 1932. I was allowed to share lunch at his table. So every noon I pushed my weight against the iron gate in

front of my benefactor's house, walked up the wide stone stairs to
the first floor, pressed with some hesitation the white bell button,
was led by a maid in a white apron to the dining room and placed by
the manufacturer's wife at the large table, beneath a painting that
depicted a collapsing stag and the dogs which were falling upon him.
Surrounded by the solid figures of my hosts, I ate without looking
up. They were kind to me, asked about my father, presented me with
sweets, and permitted me to stroke their dog: he was fat and stank.
Only once I had to eat in the kitchen when guests who resented my
presence were coming. When I pushed my weight for the last time
against the iron gate until it gave way with creaking hinges, it was
raining. I heard the rain coming down as I climbed the stone stairs.
The husband wasn't sitting at the table. He had gone hunting. They
served potato dumplings with boiled beef and horseradish. While I
was eating I heard the rain. The last piece of the potato dumplings
fell in two halves off my fork on the carpet. The wife noticed it and
looked at me. In the same moment I heard the noise of a car on the
street, then, in front of the house, braking and a scream. I saw how
the wife went to the window and rushed from the room. I ran to the
window. In the street, next to his car, stood the manufacturer in
front of the woman he had run over. As I stepped from the room into the hall, two workers carried her in and laid her on the floor; I
could see her face, the distorted mouth, the blood running from it.
Then another worker entered with the hunter's booty, hares and
partidges, which he also laid on the floor with enough distance from
the bleeding woman. I noticed how the horseradish was coming up
from my stomach. There was blood on the stone stairs. I hadn't
even reached the iron gate when I threw up.

5

My father was released with the stipulation never to show himself
again in his home county. That was in winter 1934. A two hour
walk outside our village, we waited for him on the open road that
was covered with snow. My mother carried a bundle under her arm,
his overcoat. He came, kissed me and my mother, put on the overcoat and walked the road back through the snow, hunched as if the
coat were too heavy for him. We stood on the road and looked at his
back. One could see very far in the cold air. I was five years old.

6

Since my father was without employment, my mother worked again as a seamstress. The factory was two walking hours away from the village where we had a room and an attic. The house belonged to my father's parents. Once, my mother took me along into town, to the savings bank. At a window she paid three marks. The man at the window smiled down at me and said now I would be a rich man. Then he gave the savings book to my mother. She showed me my name on the first page. As we left I saw how a man next to us stuffed into his coat pocket a fat wad of banknotes. My grandmother stood at the stove in the kitchen when I showed her the savings book. She read the amount and laughed. Three marks, she said, and threw a big piece of butter into the frying pan. She put the pan on the stove. Yes, I said, and watched the butter melt. She cut off a second, smaller piece of butter and added it. Since my father was against Hitler, I'd have to eat margarine. She took potatoes from a pot, sliced them and dropped them into the sizzling fat. A squirt got into the savings book I held in my hand. She wouldn't eat margarine, she said and: Hitler is giving us butter. She had five sons. The three younger ones were killed at the Volga river, in Hitler's war for oil and wheat. I was present when she received the first death notice. I heard her scream.

7

When Hitler ordered the freeway system to be constructed, compositions about the great project had to be written in German schools. Prizes were offered for the best ones. I told this to my father when I returned from school. He said: You don't need a prize, but two hours later: You should make an effort. He stood at the stove, threw an egg into the pan, then, already with some hesitation, a second one, and finally, after looking at it and holding it in his hand for quite a while, the third one. This will make a good meal, he said. We ate and my father said: You must write you are glad Hitler is building the freeways. Then my father, too, will surely get work again, he who was unemployed for such a long time. You must write that. After our meal, he helped me to write the composition in this manner. Then I went to play.

8

Thirteen years later, we were living in a market town in Mecklenburg, a baroness was sitting at our table, widow of a general who had been executed after the abortive assassination attempt on Hitler, of July 20, 1944, and she implored my father, the functionary of the newly founded Social Democratic Party, to help her against the land reform. He promised help.

9

In 1951, my father crossed Potsdam Square into the American sector of Berlin to dissengage himself from the war of the classes. My mother had accompanied him to Berlin, I was alone in the apartment. I was sitting next to the bookshelf reading poetry. It rained outside, while I was reading I heard the rain. I put the poetry volume down, put on a jacket and overcoat, locked the apartment door and walked through the rain to the other end of town. I discovered a tavern with a dance hall. I heard the noise from afar. When I stood at the door of the dance hall, a break was announced. So I stepped into the bar. At one of the smaller tables a woman was sitting alone, drinking beer. I sat down with her and ordered booze. We drank. After the fourth drink I touched her breast and said she had beautiful hair. Since she smiled obligingly, I ordered more booze. Next door in the dance hall the music started again, the percussion was booming, saxophones bawling, violins squealing. I pressed teeth and lips on the woman's mouth. Then I paid the check. When we stepped into the street, the rain had stopped. The moon stood white in the sky and diffused a cold light. We walked all the way in silence. A rigid smile was on the woman's face while she undressed without further ado beside the double bed in my parents' bedroom. After intercourse, I gave her cigarettes or chocolate as a present. My merely polite question: When shall we meet again? she answered with: If you please, and nearly bowed to me, or rather to the position she believed my father still to be in. He found his peace years later, in a small town in Badenia where he paid out pensions to murderers of workers and to widows of murderers of workers.

10

I saw him for the last time in the isolation ward of a hospital in Charlottenburg. I took the subway to Charlottenburg, walked down a wide street, passing ruins and tree trunks, was led at the hospital through a long bright hallway to the glass door of the isolation ward. A bell was rung. Behind the glass a nurse appeared, nodded silently when I asked for my father, walked down a long corridor and disappeared in one of the last rooms. Then my father came. He looked small in his striped pajamas which were too large for him. His slippers were dragging on the floor tiles. We stood there, the glass between us, and looked at each other. His thin face was pale. We had to raise our voices when we talked. He rattled at the locked door and called the nurse. She came, shook her head and went again. He let his arm drop, looked at me through the glass, and was silent. I heard a child screaming in one of the sickrooms. When I left, I saw him standing behind the glass door and waving. He looked old in the light that came through the large window at the end of the hallway. The train moved fast, passing rubble and construction sites. Outside was the iron gray light of a day in October.

ALONE WITH THESE BODIES
States Utopias
Grass grows
On the railway tracks
The words putrefy
On the paper
The eyes of women
Grow colder
Goodbye from tomorrow
STATUS QUO

E. L.

You came like a princess across the sea
Blown to Denmark on your flight from Danzig
On a transport by submarines chased and visited by bombers.
It seemed a sacrilege when you
Put on your glasses next to me at the movies.

Trees growing wild Roots in the riverbank's mud
Rushes green

HIS LORDSHIP
BEGS TO BE EXCUSED he'll take the early train
With Schiller you know at least it's over

TILL SOON both know it will be never

EXCUSE ME MADAM*

---

*English in the original.

YESTERDAY ON A SUNNY AFTERNOON
When I drove through the dead city of Berlin
Returned from some foreign country
I felt for the first time the desire
To exhume my wife from her graveyard
Two shovels full I threw on her myself
And to see what is still left of her
Bones which I have never seen
To hold her skull in my hand
And to imagine what her face was like
Behind the masks she had worn
Through the dead city of Berlin and other cities
When it was clothed with her flesh.

I didn't yield to my desire
Fearing the police and the gossip of my friends.

OBITUARY

She was dead when I came home. She lay in the kitchen on the tile floor, half on her belly, half on the side, one leg bent as if asleep, the head close to the door. I stooped, lifted her face out of its profile position and uttered the word I called her when we were alone. I had the feeling that I was playacting. I saw myself leaning against the door frame, partly bored, partly amused, watching a man who at three in the morning was crouched on the tile floor in his kitchen, bent over his perhaps unconscious, perhaps dead wife, who held her head in his hands and talked to her as if she was a doll for no other audience but myself. Her face was a grimace, the upper row of teeth crooked in the gaping mouth as if the jaw had been dislocated. As I lifted her up, I heard something like a groan that seemed to come rather from her guts than from her mouth, in any case from afar. I had already seen her frequently lying there as if dead when I came home and lifted her up with fear (hope) that she was dead, and the horrible sound was reassuring, an answer. Later the physician enlightened me: a kind of belch, caused by shifting her position, a remnant of breathing air, of gas squeezed from the lungs. Or something like that. I carried her to the bedroom, she was heavier than usual, naked under the housecoat. When I lowered my burden on the couch, dentures fell from her mouth. It must have come loose during the agony. Now I knew what had distorted her face. I hadn't known that she wore dentures. I went back to the kitchen and switched off the gas stove, then after a look at her empty face I picked up the telephone, thinking, receiver in hand, about my life with the dead woman, viz., about the various deaths she had sought and missed for thirteen years until today's successful night. She had tried it with a razor blade: when she was finished with one of her arteries, she called me, showed me the blood. With a rope after she locked the door but, out of hope or absent-mindedness, left open a window that could be reached from the roof. With mercury from a thermometer that she had broken for this purpose. With pills. With gas. She wanted to jump from the window or the balcony only when I was in the apartment. I called a friend, I still didn't want to acknowledge that she was dead and a matter for the authorities, then the emergency number. ARE YOU OUT OF YOUR MIND EXTINGUISH IMMEDIATELY YOUR CIGARETTE DEAD ARE YOU SURE

YES FOR TWO HOURS AT LEAST ALCOHOL THE HEART
DIDN'T YOU NOTICE THAT YOUR WIFE WHERE IS THE
LETTER WHAT LETTER DIDN'T SHE LEAVE A LETTER
WHERE WERE YOU FROM WHEN TO WHEN TOMORROW
NINE A.M. ROOM TWENTY THREE A SUMMONS THE
CORPSE WILL BE PICKED UP AUTOPSY DON'T WORRY
YOU WON'T SEE A THING. Waiting for the ambulance, a dead
woman in the next room. The irreversibility of time. Time of the
murderer: presence erased within the brackets of past and future.
Going into the next room (three times), looking at the dead woman
ONE LAST TIME (three times), she is naked under the blanket.
Growing indifference to ThatThere with which my feelings (Pain
Grief Desire) have nothing to do any more. Pulling the blanket again
over the body (three times) that will be cut open tomorrow, over the
empty face. At the third time, the first traces of poisoning: blue.
Back to the waiting room (three times). My first thought of my own
death (there is no other), at the small house in Saxony, in the tiny at-
tic I slept in, three low floors up, I five or six years old, alone around
midnight on the inevitable chamber pot, moon in the window.
HE WHO HELD THE CAT UNDER THE KNIVES OF HIS
  PLAYMATES WAS I
I THREW THE SEVENTH STONE AT THE SWALLOW'S
  NEST AND THE SEVENTH
STONE WAS THE ONE THAT HIT IT
I HEARD THE DOGS BARK IN THE VILLAGE WHEN THE
  MOON WAS
WHITE IN THE ATTIC WINDOW ASLEEP
I WAS A HUNTER OF WOLVES HUNTED WITH WOLVES
  ALONE
BEFORE FALLING ASLEEP SOMETIMES I HEARD THE
  HORSES SCREAM IN THEIR STABLES.
The feeling of the universe during the night march on a railway em-
bankment in Mecklenburg, in boots too tight and uniform too large:
the resounding emptiness. CHICKENFACE. Somewhere on the
way through the postwar world he had attached himself to me, a
skinny figure in a flapping army coat that dragged on the ground
after him, an oversize fatigue cap on the much too small bird's head,
the haversack dangling at his knees, a child in field gray. He trotted
at my side, silent, I can't remember that he said one single word,

only when I walked faster, even ran to get rid of him, he uttered small plaintive sounds between wheezing gasps. A couple of times I believed that I had lost him once and for all, he was merely a dot in the plains far behind me, then even that had disappeared; but during the dark hours he gained on me and at the latest when I woke up, in a barn or in the open, he was lying next to me, muffled in his torn coat, the bird's head near to my knees, and when I succeeded in getting up and leaving before he was awake, I soon heard him behind me with his plaintive panting. I reviled him. He stood before me, looked gratefully at me with watery dog's eyes. I don't remember any more if I spit into his face. I couldn't hit him: you don't hit a chicken. Never had I felt such a fervent desire to kill a human being. I stabbed him with the bayonet that he had dug from the recesses of his army coat to share his last tin of corned beef with me, I was the first to eat so I didn't have to taste his spittle, thrust the bayonet between his pointed shoulder blades before it was his turn, saw without regrets his blood glisten on the grass. That was at a railway embankment after I had kicked him so he would take another direction. I slew him with his infantry spade as he just had heaped a mound to protect us against the wind that blew across the plain where we had to spend the night. He didn't resist when I snatched the blade from his hand, even when he saw the balde coming down at him he didn't manage a scream. He must have expected it. He only raised his hands above his head. With relief I watched in the quickly falling darkness how a mask of black blood blotted out the chickenface. On a sunny Mayday, I pushed him off a bridge that had been blown up. I had let him walk first, he didn't look back, one push at his back was enough; the blasted gap was sixty feet wide, the bridge high enough for a fatal fall, below there was concrete. I watched his trajectory, the coat bulging like a sail, the rudder of the empty haversack, the deadly landing. Then I traversed the blasted gap: I only needed to spread my arms, borne by the air like an angel. He doesn't have a place in my dreams any more since I have killed him (three times). DREAM I walk in an old house overgrown with trees, the walls busted and held by trees, up a staircase, above which a giant woman naked with huge breasts, arms and legs spread wide apart, is suspended with ropes. (Perhaps she sustains herself in this position without any fastening: levitating.) Above me the enormous thighs, open like a pair of scissors, which I enter further with each step, the black wild bushy pubic hair, the rawness of the labia.

GERMANIA DEATH IN BERLIN

GERMANIA DEATH IN BERLIN (*Germania Tod in Berlin*) was completed in its present form in 1971, but Müller had worked on several scenes and themes of the text much earlier. The opening sequence, THE STREET 1 & 2, for instance, was written in 1956. The play's first production was at the Munich Kammerspiele, April 20, 1978, under the direction of Ernst Wendt who previously had staged the premieres of HORATIAN and HERACLES 5. It was first published in *Rotbuch # 176, Germania Tod in Berlin,* West Berlin, 1977; and in *Theater Heute Jahrbuch 1976/77.* The text has become one of Müller's frequently performed works in the West; it wasn't seen in the GDR until January 20, 1989, when a production directed by Fritz Marquardt opened at the Berliner Ensemble.

GERMANIA DEATH IN BERLIN is an early example of the dramatic structure Müller developed during the seventies, a form he called "synthetic fragment." Dispensing with a linear plot, or fable, as he would call it, he constructed performance texts out of quite disparate parts, often barely linked by a shared theme or image. The desired effect is juxtaposition rather than unity of form or content—the clash of themes, images, and structural patterns. Performers and spectators are confronted with a constant change of narrative or dramaturgic techniques and in such a way experience a content that aligns or intertwines personal interactions and emotions with history of past and present. V-effect is piled upon V-effect, so to speak, and the resulting performance is apt to evoke a wealth of associations, provided that the spectator can properly process all the images and allusions. The genre presupposes an audience that is familiar with the subject matter, and aesthetically sophisticated enough, so that it can fully read and relish the flood of complex visual and verbal signs. Nevertheless, even less initiated specatators have derived a rich and intriguing experience from these texts in performance, as many West German stagings demonstrate.

Müller's collaboration with Robert Wilson, which has surprised many critics, appears quite consistent with his concept of the synthetic fragment; Wilson employs fragmentation, visual juxtaposition, and montage, aiming at an associative rather than a narrative train of thought, an approach Müller's theatre began to explore with GERMANIA DEATH IN BERLIN. Of course, such theatre makes its demands on the audience and challenges the senses, imagination, and intellect to actively ''work'' in step with the performers on stage; Müller regards the individual spectator as the true co-creator of the event called ''performance.''

The addressee of GERMANIA DEATH IN BERLIN is clearly the East German audience. The play deals with German/Prussian history and mythology, specifically with the history and traditions of the German labor movement which supposedly has triumphed in its present incarnation as party and state of the GDR. Several topic strands can be discerned in the text's artful weave; among them, the infighting so prominent in German history and, especially, in the past and present of the German Left, for which fratricide becomes a metaphor; or the Prussian tradition of total obedience to the state and its manifestations, once welcomed and used by the new Socialist state, but now—in Müller's view—a festering trauma of the collective subconscious.

Though its designation as a ''synthetic fragment'' doesn't lead the reader to expect this, the text is most stringently constructed from its autonomous components, as the five ''sets'' of coupled scenes make evident, split in the play's center by two single scenes (THE HOLY FAMILY and THE WORKER'S MONUMENT) which comment on the ''birth'' of the two present German states without actually describing the historical moment of their constitution, a moment that, at least for the GDR, had been earlier shown in THE STREET 2.

Only one scene doesn't fit this pattern, NIGHT PIECE; with its reference to Beckett's existential theatre, it creates a metaphor of bottomless ambiguity which challenges the spectator/reader to work towards her/his own understanding of this brutal image of Man.

There are still remnants of a fable in the traditional sense, namely the story of Old Hilse, the Young Bricklayer, and his Bride, the former prostitute. When the Old Communist Hilse dies in the last scene, dreaming of ''Red flags over Rhine and Ruhr,'' (that is: West Germany), Müller is citing Gerhard Hauptmann's play, *The Weavers*, written eighty years earlier: the old weaver Hilse, accidentally shot by Prussian soldiers who crush the Silesian weaver's uprising, dies in the firm belief that God will be the final and honest judge of history. This reference appears to equate orthodox Marxism with the sectarian religion prevalent among Silesian weavers in the nineteenth century, a provocative statement that also points at the power and the problem of any Utopia.

C. W.

GERMANIA DEATH IN BERLIN
Rehearsal photo of the Berliner Ensemble production,
Berlin 1988. Scene: "Brandenburg Concerto 1."

Oda Sternberg

GERMANIA DEATH IN BERLIN
Kammerspiele, Munich, 1978. Director: Ernst Wendt.
Scene: ''The Holy Family.''

THE STREET 1
Berlin 1918

MAN: The war is over. But it kept the arm.

WOMAN: You're home, man. Things are like they used to be. Children, we've bread, you're father has come back.

MAN: Not till we own the bread and the plant, too. (*Exit. Blackout.*)

VOICE: THIS IS A GENERAL STRIKE

CHILDREN: Baker!

(*The Baker, larger than life, appears in the door of his shop.*)

CHILDREN: Bread.

BAKER: My bread won't grow from heaven. Have you dough? No dough no hunger. Do I own the world?

(*Shooting in the distance.*)

VOICE: THIS IS THE REVOLUTION

(*The baker very quickly closes his shop.*)

CHILDREN: Hey. Baker.
    (*They "shoot."*)   Dead!

(*They run in direction of the shooting. Enter the Man Who Distributes Signs, also larger than life, carrying portable signs. On the signs is written DOWN WITH SPARTAKUS.*)

SIGNS:
    What they are brewing there, it isn't your beer.
    A man a nickel. Four times four makes four
    If you carry my signs through your street.
    For Germany, if anyone should ask.

CHILD 1: I won't come with you, father is with them.

SIGNS: Number One is full. Four minus one makes three.

(*He pockets one nickel.*)

CHILD 1: My hunger comes along, it isn't me.

SIGNS: Hunger or you. As long as it's your face.

(*Children parade with signs. The shooting stops.*)

ANOTHER VOICE: LAW AND ORDER. HAS BEEN RE-ESTABLISHED.

(Light. The Baker re-opens his shop. The children step up to the Man Who Distributes Signs and hold their hands out.)

SIGNS: What do you want?
CHILDREN:　　　　The nickel.
SIGNS:　　　　What does the dog get when he barks.

(Laughs. Standing on his doorstep, the Baker joins in the laughter. Laughter continues after curtain.)

THE STREET 2
Berlin 1949

LOUDSPEAKER:
　LONG LIVE THE GERMAN DEMOCRATIC REPUBLIC
　THE FIRST WORKERSANDFARMERSSTATE ON GER-
　MAN SOIL

(Applause from loudspeaker.)

MAN: The Russian state.
ANOTHER: *(Strikes him down.)* You'll mark this day.
MAN: *(Gets up, bleeding.)*　　　　　　　　　　And you.
　(Stumbles off.)
　There are still trees in Germany, with branches.
　We'll meet again, Russian, when you are dangling.
VOICES: Stop that agent.
　　　　　　　　Stop him.
　　　　　　　　　　Where?
　　　　　　　　　　　　There.
　　　　　　　　　　　　　　Gone.
OLD MAN: *(With child riding piggyback.)*
　'Twas here we ripped the rags off the potato
　Belly of the Emperor's whore, Berlin
　And swept the Prussian tinfoil off her breast.
　The Emperor's whore, she was the workers' bride
　For one night, naked in November snow
　Bloated with hunger, badly shaken by
　The general strike, bathed in workers' blood.
　And here we stood again in January
　Hands freezing on the gun, the fog was rising
　Snow fell for seven hours, never stopped.

The bigwigs snuggles in the palace, talked.
We waited in the snow, as white as never
No soot from any smoke stack blackened it.
Soon there were less of us. In the eighth hour
You saw some throw their guns away and leave.
The bigwigs in the palace straddled chairs
And voted Karl and Rosa to the wall.
We smashed the guns against the curbstones
Crept back into the holes we lived in and
Rolled up again the sky of our hopes.
The President. A worker just like us.

VOICE 1: A worker just like us. Where is my palace.

VOICE 2: They won't know their own mother anymore.

ONEARM: You're eating shit.

MAN 1:   But not from anyone.

(*Pause.*)

ONEARM: Are you still Germans?

MAN 2:   Do you have one arm
Too many?

(*Pause.*)

ONEARM: Smolensk, Comrade. Next time we'll do better.

(*Pause.*)

MAN 3: It is the head. He's got one head too many.

MAN 1: A funny bird.

MAN 2:   He's looking for a cage.

MAN 3: Happy-go-lucky. Bird, you are in luck.
There goes a cage, he's looking for a bird.

(*Exit Onearm. A Trench Coat.*)

TRENCH COAT: Where did he go.

MAN 1:   Who.

MAN 2:   Someone here?

MAN 3:   No one.

(*Exit Trench Coat. Windbreakers on bicycles.*)

WINDBREAKER 1: Throwing their weight around. Pedestrians.
In line for handouts without ration cards?

MAN: National holiday, Son. Don't you like it?

WINDBREAKER 1: What nation?

MAN 2:   Yours it isn't.

WINDBREAKER 2:   Do you notice
Any nation here?

(*Tears down a flag and dances on it. Two Trench Coats.*)

MAN: They're drunk.

TRENCH COATS: (*Rip open the windbreakers of the Windbreakers.
Leaflets drop on the ground.*)
                        From this.

(*They take the Windbreakers away. Two Gentlemen with suitcases.*)

GENTLEMAN 1: Do you hear the grass growing? That's the tundra. The tundra is coming. That's what's tickling your feet. Do
you see my shoes: green. Hurry, or the grass will catch up with
us.

(*Exit. Three Whores. A Pimp.*)

PIMP: The street is crawling with customers. Why ain't you working?

WHORE 1: National holiday, sweetie.

PIMP: They'll fuck under any government.

WHORE 2: They won't fuck me much longer. Come spring, I'll
beat it.

(*Pimp tries to beat her.*)

WHORE 1: The fuzz.

(*Exit Pimp. The Whores laugh.*)

WHORE 1: I'll still take my fat guy to the cleaners. A hosiery
plant in Saxony. He won't do it much longer, three times already
People's Control checked his joint. The missis is getting nosy,
too. I still want to get a mink out of him.

WHORE 3: (*Jeeringly.*) That rag I'd like to see.

WHORE 1: The blond at the precinct told me he's got to marry
me if I'm not off the street soon so he won't have to write reports
on me.

(*Sings:*) ONCE THERE WAS A HUSSAR TRUE

WHORE 3: Marry. A cop.

WHORE 1: I like the blond.

WHORE 3: That's the pits. (*Spits.*)

WHORE 1: You of all people, walking the streets since World War One.

WHORE 3: Scum.

WHORE 1: After you. (*They fight. Policeman.*)

POLICEMAN: A quarrel, ladies?

WHORE 3: No way, Commissioner, Sir.

WHORE 1: You must have taken us for someone else.

WHORE 2: If it's the eyes, go and see ANSORG. (*Exit Policeman.*)

WHORE 3: They're everywhere. I'll go to Ku'damm.

WHORE 1: They're waiting for you, you skeleton.

WHORE 3: I'll tear your mug to shreds.

(*A Policeman walks by. Whore 2 and Whore 3 leave.*)

WHORE 2: Won't you come along.

WHORE 1: I'll stay. I like it here.

(*Exit Whores 2 and 3. A Drunk.*)

DRUNK: (*Sings.*) OH THE JOYS OF THE FOREST
Hey, doll!

YOUNG MAN: Leave that woman alone.

DRUNK: (*Staggering on.*) OH HOW LONESOME FEELS MY BREAST

YOUNG MAN: Shall we walk, together?

WHORE 1: Today is a holiday. Today I'll walk alone.

BRANDENBURG CONCERTO 1
Circus Ring. 2 Clowns.

CLOWN 1: I am the King of Prussia. I have built myself a palace in this beautiful countryside because I like it here and so that I can serve my people better since I have hemorrhoids and rheumatism from all those wars I had to conduct in Silesia, Bohemia, and Saxony, for the honor of Prussia, and which are very famous.

CLOWN 2: I want to be King of Prussia, too.

CLOWN 1: You are the miller of Potsdam.

CLOWN 2: Do I also have hemorrhoids.

CLOWN 1: (*Grandly.*) Did you fight my battles.

CLOWN 2: (*Intimidated.*)

CLOWN 1: Your windmill stands next to my palace. It clatters all day long. It disturbs me, of course, when I govern. And while I play the flute which I love very much to do and am a master of.

CLOWN 2: It doesn't disturb me. I also can play the flute. (*Grabs his crotch.*)

CLOWN 1: I only play serious music. Of course, I could build myself another palace in another countryside. After all, I am the King of Prussia. I only need to conquer England, for instance, which would be chicken feed for me, as you'd admit, and I could build my palace in England. But I want it here, in my beloved Prussia, in this countryside which I like so very much.

CLOWN 2: This is my windmill. I won't allow that my windmill is taken away from me. If I can't keep my windmill, I won't play with you.

CLOWN 1: That is fine. Since I have decided to confront certain rumors which my enemies have spread because my glory won't let them sleep, as I am an example for all the world since I speak French and am very enlightened.

CLOWN 2: (*Slyly.*) How does the babe get in the belly. That's simple. But how does it not get in the belly.

CLOWN 1: That is a philosophical question. I don't have the time for it now. I am the first servant of my state.

CLOWN 2: (*Drops his pants.*) My state is bigger than yours. Are you doing it with the right or the left hand.

CLOWN 1: That is none of your business. Pull your pants up or I'll call the ringmaster.

CLOWN 2: (*Horrified, grabs his behind and quickly pulls his pants up again.*)

CLOWN 1: I have no sense of humor in politics. I am the first servant of my state.

CLOWN 2: (*Laughs and, horrified, claps his hand over his mouth.*)

CLOWN 1: Therefore, even if it breaks my heart, and it will break my heart, I am sure of it, I shall come to you, the King of Prussia to the miller of Potsdam, and give you an order that you shall set up your windmill at some other place since it disturbs me when I govern and when I play the flute. Yet, you wouldn't let yourself be intimidated but stand up to me as a true German man and say right into my face that you have a trade license and a building permit and that you don't want to set up your windmill elsewhere even if I am King of Prussia three times over because there are still judges in Berlin and your windmill is going to stay where it is next to my palace, though it clatters all day long and disturbs my government for which I need utmost concentration since I have to do everything myself because no dog in Prussia is going to piss without my express permission and I love animals as I do my playing the flute which I love very much and am a master of, however, a King is no human being but the first servant of his state, (*Clown 2 laughs and, horrified, claps his hand over his mouth.*) and if it breaks his heart and it will break my heart. I am sure of it. (*Weeps.*) Do you remember everything I said?

CLOWN 2: The lion.

(*Enter a lion. Clown 2 grabs a trapeze that is lowered from the flies. Clown 1 grabs Clown 2 and climbs up at him. Clown 2 is ticklish and, shaken by fits of laughter, he lets go of the trapeze. They fall down on the lion who breaks into two parts which exit in opposite directions. The trapeze disappears into the flies.*)

CLOWN 1: Now we have broken the lion.

CLOWN 2: You have broken the lion.

CLOWN 1: You did let go.

CLOWN 2: Because you tickled me.

(*Pause. Clown 1 is thinking.*)

CLOWN 1: We'll simply say the lion wasn't here.

CLOWN 2: They won't believe us.

(*Pause. Clown 1 is thinking.*)

CLOWN 1: We'll say lions don't exist.

CLOWN 2: Yes, that's good.

CLOWN 1: Now we'll start.

CLOWN 2: And where is my windmill.

CLOWN 1: You've got to imagine it. I have to imagine my palace too. Don't you have any imagination.

CLOWN 2: No. I know what I'll do. I'm going to play the miller and the windmill, too.

CLOWN 1: That isn't permitted. Anyone could play a windmill, but how should I play my palace. A palace can only be imagined.

CLOWN 2: And it is much more beautiful for it.

CLOWN 1: (*Beaming.*) Yes, that is true.

(*Enter the Ringmaster with his whip.*)

RINGMASTER: What have you done with the lion.
CLOWN 2: (*Hides behind Clown 1.*)
CLOWNS 1 & 2: Lions don't exist.

(*The Ringmaster's jaw drops to the ground. He picks it up and exits, looking around bashfully.*)

CLOWN 1: Now we'll begin. First we'll do government. Where is my chair.

(*Chair from the flies, Clown 1 proceeds to sit down, Clown 2 sneaks up behind him, pulls the chair away, Clown 1 doesn't sit down, stands erect again.*)

CLOWN 1: Stop. We've forgotten something. My whippet. I can't govern without my whippet.
CLOWN 2: Your whippet?
CLOWN 1: Yes. Where is my whippet.

(*Dog from the flies.*)

CLOWN 2: Haha. That's supposed to be a whippet. That is a dog.
CLOWN 1: (*Sternly.*) A whippet is a dog. The chair is too far upstage.
CLOWN 2: You are too far downstage.
CLOWN 1: Yes. The chair is too far upstage and I am too far downstage.
CLOWN 2: I know what we'll do. You'll go upstage and I'll carry the chair downstage.
CLOWN 1: Yes, that's good. (*They do it.*)
CLOWN 1: Now the chair is too far downstage and I am too far upstage.
CLOWN 2: We didn't do it right. I have to carry the chair upstage and you must go downstage.
CLOWN 1: Yes.

(*The chair disappears into the flies.*)

CLOWN 1: The chair is gone.
CLOWN 2: Yes, I can't see it either anymore.
CLOWN 1: I'll sit down on you, you are my chair.
CLOWN 2: And who'll be the windmill.

CLOWN 1: One thing at a time.

(*Clown 2 goes down on hands and knees, Clown 1 sits on him.*)

CLOWN 1: Now I'll govern and you must clatter.

(*Clown 2 gets up, Clown 1 falls down.*)

CLOWN 1: You can't simply get up while I'm governing.
CLOWN 2: Now I'm the windmill. You simply have to imagine the chair.
CLOWN 1: Yes.

(*Clown 1 sits in the air.*)

CLOWN 2: THE WINDMILL IT CLATTERS AT THE WHIS-PERING BROOK
CLITTER CLATTER CLITTER CLATTER CLITTER CLAT-TER
CLOWN 1: I can't imagine the chair any longer.
CLOWN 2: Why don't you govern standing.
CLOWN 1: It won't work. I think I'll stop governing. It is too difficult. We'll now do Playing-the-Flute.
CLOWN 2: Shall we play with my flute or shall we play with your flute. I know what we'll do; you'll play with my flute and I'll play with your flute.
CLOWN 1: You don't have a flute, you are the miller of Potsdam. Begin.
CLOWN 2: I am the miller of Potsdam. The King of Prussia is my neighbor. My windmill stands next to his palace. I have been told that my windmill disturbs the King of Prussia when he governs and while he plays the flute because it clatters all day long, and he intends to come and see me, the King of Prussia the miller of Potsdam, and give an order that I shall set up my windmill elsewhere. But he'll come to the wrong guy. Because I have a trade license, and a building permit I have also. Yessir. (*Clown 1 applauds.*) Just let him come, that fucker of assholes, with his whippet and his crooked stick. I'll teach him a lesson. There are still judges in Berlin. Yessir. (*Clown 1 applauds.*) I'll put his whippet through the meat grinder and make kindling wood from his stick. (*Clown 1 applauds.*) I'll rip his asshole wide open, I am a German man. Yessir. (*Clown 1 applauds.*) What's that supposed to mean: King. Anyone could govern—

CLOWN 1: Stop. You must remain within the bounds of legality.

CLOWN 2: What's that?

CLOWN 1: That's French and it means IT IS FORBIDDEN TO DUMP REFUSE. Now, my entrance.

(*Clown 1 stumbles over his crooked stick and falls on his face.*)

CLOWN 2: Do you always enter on your nose.

CLOWN 1: I am the King of Prussia, my palace stands next to your windmill, and I order you, Miller of Potsdam, to set up your windmill somewhere else because it clatters all day long which disturbs me when I govern and play the flute.

CLOWN 2: I am the miller of Potsdam. (*His knees begin to tremble. He tries to steady them with his hands.*) I am a German man. (*Falls down, gets up again while the crooked stick threatens him, falls down again.*)

CLOWN 1: (*Raising the stick.*) If you don't play your part now, I'll tell the Ringmaster that you broke the lion. I know you. You are doing this only to embarrass me in front of all these people, it's sheer malice.

CLOWN 2: (*Gets up again and falls down again. On hands and knees.*) Most decidedly not. I'm really trying. Just see how I'm sweating. It simply overwhelms me. I can't do anything about it. It's pulling my feet from under me. It's coming from within me. It is a force of Nature.

CLOWN 1: (*Angry.*) I'll teach you what that is, a force of Nature. (*Beats him.*) I am the first servant of my state.

(*Clown 2 licks the crooked stick and begins to devour it. Eating the stick, he gets up with its help until he stands erect, stiff like a stick. Martial music that turns into the thunder of battle. The backdrop opens and reveals a conflagration, blurbs are rising from it: EACH SHOT A FROG   EACH KICK A BRIT   EACH THRUST A RUSS. Clown 2 marches goose-stepping into the fire.*)

CLOWN 1: Actually, I had imagined it differently since I speak French and am very enlightened. But this will work too, of course.

(*The dog, also goose-stepping, follows Clown 2.*)

CLOWN 1: (*To the dog.*) ET TU, BRUTE!

BRANDENBURG CONCERTO 2

Palace. A buffet supper. An Empire chair. Backstage a choir, singing: WHEN THE PEOPLE TOOK POSSESSION OF THE POWERPLANT.

A COMRADE: (*Introducing.*) This is the bricklayer from Stalin Avenue. "Hero of Labor," as of today. Take the caviar, Comrade, you won't get it anywhere else. You've paid for it with your Stalin Avenue. He gave Frederick The One And Only marching orders, from Berlin to Potsdam, since he was blocking the sun for us Unter Den Linden. With four men, for three times less money than those experts from the West had estimated, and in world record time. But he is new at the buffet supper. What would you like. If we spoon cabbage soup with our populace, they'll make chopped meat of us; this is Germany, Comrade. Dictatorship of the Proletariat, even in the kitchen. Eating is party work. The red one is better.

(*Exit. The Bricklayer, his head bandaged, eats. President.*)

PRESIDENT: Today is your day, Comrade. You look as if
   It lasts too long for you.
BRICKLAYER: It's long enough.
PRESIDENT: Your head?
BRICKLAYER: A thank you from the working class.
   They tried to recast me as a monument.
   Materials came down from the fifth floor.
   And if you pin another medal upon me
   You soon might set me up as deputy
   Of Old Fritz, the King, Unter Den Linden.
PRESIDENT: The stones they use to pelt us with today
   Will fit into new walls tomorrow, Comrade.
   What else is ailing you.
BRICKLAYER: The buffet supper.
PRESIDENT: You'll have to get familiar with it. I
   Have learned it, too.
COMRADE: Comrade President
   The artists have arrived.
PRESIDENT: I have to do
   My number.

(Exit. Music. The Brandenburg Concerto. Bricklayer sits on the Empire chair.)

BRICKLAYER: Just the chair for my behind.

(Frederick the Second of Prussia as a vampire.)

FREDERICK II: Won't he get up, lout, when his King is here.

BRICKLAYER: I thought he wouldn't need a chair no more.
I'll teach you where God lives.
(Attacks Frederick the Second who strikes him with his stick.)
Hey, that's my back.
(Breaks the stick over his knee. Frederick the Second attacks him from behind.)
You've got the wrong guy, sweetie. Fuck your dog.
(Shakes him off. Frederick the Second goes for his throat.)
Are you still thirsty, beast. Go and drink water.
(Struggle. Enter Comrade with a tray. Frederick the Second vanishes.)

COMRADE: That's from the President. Pork chops and beer.
So you won't spoil your stomach here before
You are familiar with a buffet supper.

BRICKLAYER: *(Eats the pork chop and drinks the beer.)*

HOMMAGE À STALIN 1

Snow. Battle noise. Three Soldiers. Their bodies aren't complete anymore. Enter, in the snowstorm, a Young Soldier.

SOLDIER 1: Here come fresh supplies.

SOLDIER 2: He still has everything.

SOLDIER 3: Who's next.

SOLDIER 1: I.

SOLDIER 2: Comrade, wherefrom?

YOUNG SOLDIER: The battle.

SOLDIER 3: Comrade, whereto?

YOUNG SOLDIER: Where there is no battle.

SOLDIER 1: Comrade, your hand.

(Tears off his arm. The Young Soldier screams. The dead laugh and begin gnawing away at the arm.)

SOLDIER 3: *(Offering the arm.)* Aren't you hungry?

(*The Young Soldier hides his face with his remaining hand.*)

SOLDIER 1: Next time it's your turn. There is meat for all of us in this pocket.

VOICES: Vive l'empereur.

Long live the Emperor.

SOLDIER 1: That is Napoleon. He is coming every third night. (*Napoleon walks by. He looks pale and bloated. He drags behind him a soldier of his Grand Army by the feet.*) That's alright. They are his corpses. They wouldn't be here without him. And he is keeping count, he is a skinflint. Only with us you'll find comradeship. You really won't eat? (*Behind Napoleon, Caesar has appeared, his face green, his toga bloodied and torn.*) The green one behind him is Caesar. He had it coming, twenty-three holes.

SOLDIER 2: If you don't count the asshole. (*Laughter.*)

SOLDIER 1: He lives from panhandling. His corpses are tied up in a frozen account: his battlefields are too far below.

SOLDIER 3: Why didn't he put some on the side, that greaseball.

SOLDIER 1: Sometimes, Napoleon throws him a leg. (*Laughs.*) Or an arm. (*Throws the cleanly picked arm at Caesar.*) No one needs to go hungry with us. (*Caesar picks up the arm and vanishes in the snowstorm. The Young Soldier runs off, screaming.*)

SOLDIER 3: He'll be back. The pocket is watertight.

(*More and more soldiers stagger or crawl on stage, fall down, remain on the ground. Then enter, larger than life, the Nibelungs: Gunther, Hagen, Volker, and Gernot.*)

GUNTHER: (*Stalking around the corpses.*) Malingerers.

Shirkers. Defeatists. Yellow-bellied scum.

VOLKER: They think once they kicked the bucket they've done all they could be called to do.

HAGEN: (*Scornfully.*) They think they are out of it.

GERNOT: They'll be amazed.

GUNTHER: Take up your swords, all of you Nibelungs
The Huns are coming back. IN GOD WE TRUST.
(*The Nibelungs arm themselves with corpses, or limbs of corpses, and hurl them yelling at imaginary Huns so that an irregular mound of corpses is created.*)
See, Attila, the harvest our swords reaped.

(The Nibelungs sit on the mound of corpses, take off their helmets, and drink beer from skulls.)

GERNOT: Always the same routine.

(The others look at him, they are upset.)

I'm not saying I won't play anymore. But what is it all about, actually.

VOLKER: Did you already forget Siegfried whom the Huns in Odenwald forest . . .

HAGEN: *(Lifts his skull.)* Revenge for Siegfried.

GUNTHER AND VOLKER: *(In same manner.)* Revenge for Siegfried.

GERNOT: *(To Hagen.)* But I've seen it with my own two eyes. I mean, everybody knows you did . . .

GUNTHER: We all have seen how Hagen pulled the spear from the wound after the Huns from their hiding place . . .

GERNOT: I saw who threw the spear.

GUNTHER: He was a traitor.

GERNOT: Who.

GUNTHER: Siegfried. I actually never intended to tell you this. Youth should be allowed to cherish illusions, as long as it's absolutely possible. Now you know.

GERNOT: I still don't know why we keep scuffling with the Huns here.

VOLKER: Are you a Hun who needs a reason to fight.

HAGEN: Because we can't get out of this pocket, that's why we keep scuffling with the Huns.

GERNOT: But we only need to stop and there won't be a pocket anymore.

GUNTHER: Did he say: stop.

VOLKER: He'll never learn.

GUNTHER: We mustn't lose hope. He isn't a Hun.

VOLKER: Sure, we'll make him shape up.

HAGEN: Anyway, we'll have to start now. Time is money.

(The three get up, arm themselves, and move in on Gernot. He jumps up.)

GERNOT: I won't die each and every night. It's boring. I don't enjoy it. I'd like to do something else, for a change. That thing with women, for instance. I've forgotten what its called.

HAGEN: (*Scornfully.*) He has forgotten what it's called.

VOLKER: That is today's youth for you. No ideals anymore.

GUNTHER: Why do you think your mother gave birth to you. We are going to rehearse it until you'll know it in your sleep.

(*The three Nibelungs, in a protracted fight, hack the fourth one to pieces. Then they masturbate together.*)

VOLKER: (*Masturbating.*) "I'd like to do something else, for a change. That thing with women, for instance. I've forgotten what it's called." (*The Nibelungs laugh.*)

HAGEN: (*In similar fashion.*) I don't even know anymore what that is, a woman. I believe I wouldn't find the hole anymore. (*The Nibelungs laugh.*)

GUNTHER: (*In similar fashion.*) War is men's business. Anyway, now the money needs only to be split in three. And we'll find the hole in the pocket, don't worry. (*The Nibelungs laugh.*)

VOLKER: (*Tunes his violin.*)

GUNTHER: Leave your violin out of this. I know your tricks. He wants to soften us with his song-and-dance routine. SLEEP LIT-TLE PRINCE SLEEP TIGHT. And then he'll take a beeline and stash all the boodle away for himself.

HAGEN: Better, we take care of him right away.

GUNTHER: Let's go. (*They arm themselves.*)

VOLKER: Comrades.

(*They hack him to pieces.*)

GUNTHER: Now it's only the two of us.

HAGEN: One too many.

(*They hack each other to pieces. A moment of silence. The battle noise also has stopped. Then the limbs and other parts of corpses crawl towards each other and—with a terrible din of metallic sounds, screams, fragmented singing—they form a monster from scrap metal and human debris. The din carries over into the next scene.*)

HOMMAGE À STALIN 2

Tavern. Sound of factory whistles. Bells ringing.
Innkeeper. Two men from the lower middle classes. A figure: The
Salesman of Skulls.

MIDDLECLASS 1: Stalin is dead.
MIDDLECLASS 2: It took him long enough.
INNKEEPER: Watch out.

(*Three Whores.*)

MIDDLECLASS 1: How about us two, young lady.
WHORE 3: Go home, kiddie. Mama's crying.
WHORE 2: Do you have permission to stay up that late.
WHORE 1: There ain't no mothers anymore.
MIDDLECLASS 1: Why not in black, ladies, on a day like this.
WHORE 2: With us, it's down under. (*Shows her black lingerie.*)
MIDDLECLASS 2: A beer for our widows and orphans.
WHORE 1: We drink only bubbly.
INNKEEPER: You're not on Ku'damm here.
WHORE 3: Well, since it's you.

(*Beer.*)

MIDDLECLASS 1: Bubbly. An honest craft lays the foundation
for prosperity.
MIDDLECLASS 2: Rather an honest hole, if you'd ask me.
INNKEEPER: A prosperous one.
WHORE 2: (*To Middleclass 1.*) We don't work manually, Mister.
MIDDLECLASS 1: No insult intended, Madam. I'm a humble
craftsman myself.
WHORE 2: Phooey.
MIDDLECLASS 1: The tongue works faster than the hand.
(*Laughs.*)
WHORE 3: Don't choke on it, sonny.
WHORE 2: (*Points at the figure.*) Who's that ghost there. Hoooh!
WHORE 1: (*Waits for an effect but there is none.*) He didn't stir.
MIDDLECLASS 2: Maybe it's a monument.
WHORE 1: That's Haarmann. You see the bag under his chair.
He again dismembered a guy and in his bag there, he's got the
pieces. Where his jacket is bulging, that's where the knife is.

MIDDLECLASS 2: With the price of meat, I'd nearly call it self-defense.

MIDDLECLASS 1: I wouldn't like to know how many I've already eaten.

WHORE 3: It couldn't be Haarmann. He looks different, more chubby. I've seen him. It was last Tuesday. He already had his knife out. Man, did I scream. And gone he was, like a shadow.

MIDDLECLASS 1: You've seen a ghost, lady. Haarmann is in Heaven.

WHORE 2: That's a deaf-mute.

WHORE 3: Anyway, I won't go home alone tonight.

MIDDLECLASS 1: (*Flips open a pocket-knife.*) How would you like it.

WHORE 3: (*Squeals.*)

(*Enter four Bricklayers.*)

FAT BRICKLAYER: He won't drink beer no more.

GENERAL: Let's celebrate.

YOUNG BRICKLAYER: What do you try to tell us, General.

GENERAL: What I have said. Beer.

HILSE: Be glad, General
The Russians made you do construction work.

GENERAL: I've only done my duty as a German.

HILSE: I'd made you face the firing squad, all of you.

GENERAL: We'll see who'll sooner face the firing squad.

YOUNG BRICKLAYER: (*To Whore.*) That's her. It will be four years in October.
I've looked for you all over. How are you doing?

WHORE 2: Who is that guy there you have roped in, girl.

MIDDLECLASS 2: Four years. He must be in a hurry.

MIDDLECLASS 1: (*Sings.*) ROSEMARIE. ROSEMARIE.
SEVEN YEARS MY HEART CRIED FOR THEE.

WHORE 2:   Young man
I think you're whistling up the wrong tree here.

YOUNG BRICKLAYER: What, for instance, are your plans to-night.

WHORE 2: He won't listen. Love must be wonderful.

HILSE: Don't touch them, boy. That's not your cup of tea.

WHORE 1: I don't believe that I'll have time tonight.

YOUNG BRICKLAYER: You're waiting here for a Capitalist.
WHORE 3: That would be great.
WHORE 1:   I'm going.
YOUNG BRICKLAYER: We'll go together.

(*Exit Whore 1, alone.*)

MIDDLECLASS 1: Must be a virgin. (*Middleclass 1 and Middleclass 2 laugh.*)
YOUNG BRICKLAYER: (*To Whore 3 and Whore 2.*) So she's got a guy.
MIDDLECLASS 1: Oh, don't ever ask me, Lohengrin.
MIDDLECLASS 2: He can only count to number one.
WHORE 3: (*Cries.*) That's true love.

(*Young Bricklayer leaves. Hilse tries to hold him back.*)

YOUNG BRICKLAYER: I don't need a guardian.

(*Young Bricklayer pushes Hilse back.*)

GENERAL: (*Laughs.*)
FAT BRICKLAYER: It's none of your business.
GENERAL: The model worker.

(*Model Worker, his head bandaged, sits down at the bricklayers' table. The bricklayers move to another table.*)

GENERAL: Great head.
FAT BRICKLAYER: They tell me there are certain people
     As soon as they pass any building site
     Bricks will come dropping down.
MODEL WORKER: What's eating you?
MIDDLECLASS 1: (*Drunk.*) I say we'll have a war. And you?
MIDDLECLASS 2: (*In similar fashion.*) Who cares.
WHORE 3 AND 2: (*Sing.*)
     AND ALL OF US WE'LL GO TO PARADISE

(*Whores and Middleclass Men exit singing.*)

GENERAL: Maybe, some things will soon be changing here
     And soon some people won't have much to laugh at.

(*Pause.*)

FAT BRICKLAYER: Germans can take a lot. But not forever.

(*Pause.*)

HILSE: What do you want to tell us, General.

GENERAL: I'm smelling human flesh, said the giant.

(*Exit. The Fat Bricklayer follows him.*)

MODEL WORKER: Nice people.

HILSE: Not as nice as your sort is.

MODEL WORKER: I've been told once that you are a Red. (*Pause.*)

HILSE: I'm not a traitor of my fellow workers. (*Exit.*)

MODEL WORKER: Pour me another shot. I'm going to need it
When I come home tonight. I hardly dare
To go home. Each night there is something new.
The carpet yesterday. Today the BUFFET.
A medal, that's what they have pinned on me.
And now my wife, she plays the lady since
I'm in all the papers.

INNKEEPER: Noblesse oblige.

MODEL WORKER: Had I but known the price a bonus cost me.

(*Pause. A drunk.*)

INNKEEPER: You've had enough.

DRUNK: I'm a free citizen.

INNKEEPER: And this is my place.

DRUNK: I was already left
When your place was a Nazi joint, brown with
Storm Troopers.
(*Sits down with the Model Worker.*)
Buy me a drink, Comrade.
You are a working stiff like me. We must
Stick together against Capital.
Against Socialism, too. I was
A member, C.Y.L., since '24.
Nobody can fool me. In Stalingrad
They've cooked me tender. That was more than war.
We would have eaten grass. But I did not
See any grass. We didn't ask a bone
If it came from a horse, or rather: I
ONCE HAD A GOOD COMRADE.
But man gets used to everything. Who's sitting
Here: I was the only N.C.O.
Who was commander of a company.

The Captain croaked, and the Lieutenants too.
We got finally out of the pocket
All of us twenty four, except for ten.
I got them safely out. I was alright.
And my boys, they were alright like me.
MODEL WORKER: You ought to know.
DRUNK: Oh yes, and just today
I've met one. He's with the government
State-Secretary, or what they call it now.
That boy has got it made: Way up he is.
But right away he recognized me. You, Boss?
Always the same, says I. And he: Come on
Let's celebrate. I went along. His wife
Spit fire when we tried to reconstruct
With beer on her parquet floor our pocket
Of Stalingrad. He locked her in the kitchen.
And then we reconstructed our pocket.
And after the fourth bottle I ask: Could you
Still crawl on elbows, Willi, you old pig.
And what shall I tell you, you won't believe this:
He could, and how. That well I drilled them boys.
(*Spills beer on the table.*)
This is the Volga. Here is Stalingrad.
MODEL WORKER: That is my beer
DRUNK: You aren't interested.
The war, it isn't over. It just began.
It won't scratch me no more. I've seen the world's
asshole, inside and out. (*Exit.*)

(*The Young Bricklayer and Whore 1.*)

YOUNG BRICKLAYER: (*To the Model Worker.*) That's a girl!
Hey, model worker, you've got your pockets stuffed
With our money for your red overtime.
MODEL WORKER: In time you'll learn your lesson.
YOUNG BRICKLAYER: Not from you.
We need a place to live.
WHORE 1:   You're in a hurry.
YOUNG BRICKLAYER: No goofing on the job now any longer
Could be I'm working at my own apartment.
MODEL WORKER: I've told you right away you'll learn your

Explosion of a Memory 65

lesson.

YOUNG BRICKLAYER: I don't need your advice.

MODEL WORKER: There will be others.

WHORE 1: (*Sings.*) AS SWEET AS NOW IT SHALL FOREVER BE
I think now I had one too much.

YOUNG BRICKLAYER: Let's go.
I'll take you home.

WHORE 1: I've got to work.

YOUNG BRICKLAYER: Night shift?

WHORE 1: Yes. I'm always on the night shift.

(*The Salesman of Skulls has gotten up, he picks up his bag and approaches, tottering a bit.*)

WHORE 1: What's he up to.

YOUNG BRICKLAYER: That's Santa Claus. Are you alright, Mister?

SALESMAN OF SKULLS: A beautiful couple. Allow me to offer you a little souvenir. (*Pulls a skull from his bag. Whore 1 squeals.*) A memento mori for your new home. IN THE MIDST OF LIFE WE ARE / IN THE EMBRACE OF DEATH. I personally have dug this one up. And cooked it three times. A clean specimen. 18th century, according to the tombstone. And it's an excellent skull, just feel its temple. The earth brings it all to the light of day. Thoughts have been created here, Sir, the theodicy of our great Leibniz had enough space in this cavity. Materialism is a mistake, believe me.

WHORE 1: (*Laughs.*) He is funny.

SALESMAN OF SKULLS: You could also buy a skeleton. A philosophical clothes tree. Take your coat off, Madam. That much, Sir? A skeleton, of course, is more expensive. It's hard to find a complete skeleton. Who knows what the dead are doing with their bones. (*Giggles.*) Well, I have my suspicions. Enough of this. Fifty for the skull.

WHORE 1: I'm afraid.

YOUNG BRICKLAYER: I'll take care of it.

SALESMAN OF SKULLS: It's a steal, Sir. We're not talking Reichsmark. It's barely covering expenses.

YOUNG BRICKLAYER: Put your junk back, Boss.

WHORE 1: I'd like to go.

SALESMAN OF SKULLS: Beg your pardon. (*Whore and Young*

Bricklayer exit.) I'd love to drink one or two glasses more of your delicious liquor but, unfortunately, I'm not liquid anymore. Would you take the skull as security.

INNKEEPER: And it will be redeemed on doomsday, right. It's your business if you want to drink one or two more, but I'd like to see cash.

MODEL WORKER: Are you also personally killing them, Colleague?

SALESMAN OF SKULLS: (*Sits at the Model Worker's table.*)
I'm working foundations. So to speak. We're moving cemeteries, unbeknownst to the public. Reburying, as it's called in the language of the bereaved. I am a bereaved person, I'm reburying. UNDER FLOWERS AND GRASS. We work nights. Under the influence, because we're in danger of being contaminated. EVEN IF SWEETHEART IS AFRAID OF THE DEAD. An activity of some piquancy, as far as I'm concerned: I used to be an historian. A case of mistaken judgment of historical periods, the Thousand Year Reich, you'll understand. Since history has referred me to cemeteries, to their theological aspects, so to speak, I've become immunized against the ptomaine of secular promises. The Golden Age is in the past. Jesus is the afterbirth of the dead.
Do you know Virgil.
WITH A NEW BREED OF MEN SENT DOWN
   FROM HEAVEN
THE IRON SHALL CEASE, THE GOLDEN RACE
   ARISE
AND FREE THE EARTH FROM NEVER CEASING
   FEAR.
THEY SHALL REIGN OVER A WORLD AT
   PEACE
FIRST SHALL THE EARTH, UNTILLED, POUR FREELY
   FORTH
CARESSING FLOWERS. THE PLAIN BY SLOW
   DEGREES
WITH WAVING CORN-CROPS SHALL TO GOLDEN
   GROW
FROM THE WILD BRIAR SHALL HANG THE BLUSHING
   GRAPE
AND STUBBORN OAKS SWEAT HONEY DEW.

NO NEED
SHALL LURK THERE, BIDDING TEMPT THE DEEP WITH
SHIPS
GIRD TOWNS WITH WALLS, WITH FURROWS CLEAVE
THE EARTH.

INNKEEPER: Gentlemen, get your asses off my chairs. Closing time.

THE HOLY FAMILY

Führerbunker. Hitler, frozen in one of his poses. A bell strikes midnight. Hitler stirs, yawns, makes a few steps, tries his poses, drinks gasoline from a can, etc.

HITLER: Joseph!

(*Goebbels, with clubfoot and enormous breasts, very pregnant.*)

GOEBBELS: My Führer!

HITLER: (*Taps on Goebbels' pregnant belly.*) How is our guarantor doing. Is he moving? Good. Are you drinking your gasoline? (*Squeezes Goebbels' nipples.*) Is the udder brimming as it befits a German mother? Good. Farms and arms.

GOEBBELS: We have only a three-day supply of gasoline left.

HITLER: So hurry the delivery. Guard! (*Guard in black uniform with a boar's head. While pinching the behind of giggling Goebbels.*) My breakfast! (*Exit Guard. A Soldier. Hitler eats him, the head last. Sneezes, spits, and picks hairs from his mouth.*) I gave orders that my men are to be shaved before I eat them. Disgusting! (*Sneezes and drinks gasoline.*)

GOEBBELS: May I draw attention to the fact, my Führer, that we have to keep the group of men with top-secret clearance small. The German people love you as a vegetarian. We have problems with our staff, the barber can't produce proof of Aryan descent. The previous one has been detailed for other duty, he is shaving Mr. Stalin. The ways of Providence are miraculous.

HITLER: (*Yells.*) Deceit. Malice. Treason. I'm surrounded with traitors. They are planning to kill me. They are planting bombs in my bed. They are throwing knives into my food. They are putting poison in my gasoline. I'll chop their heads off. I'll string them up. I'll quarter them. (*Howls, bites the carpet, always howling. Crawls up to Goebbels, puts his head on his breasts, cries.*)

GOEBBELS: (*Caresses and rocks him.*) You are the greatest. You are stronger than all of them. They can't harm you. You'll punish them.

HITLER: (*Still in the previous position.*) Yes. Chop off fingers. Hands. Arms. Legs. Cut off nose. (*Giggling and wriggling.*) Rip off prick.

GOEBBELS: (*Wags his finger.*) It isn't nice to say prick.

HITLER: (*Throws himself on the ground, kicking.*) You've said prick. Admit that you've said prick. Traitor. You too are a traitor.

GOEBBELS: (*Quickly.*) I've said prick. I'm admitting it. Mercy, my Führer.

HITLER: (*Gets up, strikes Napoleon's famous pose.*) You see. Now you've got to lick my boots for it. (*Goebbels throws himself at Hitler's left boot.*) First the right one. (*Goebbels throws himself at the right boot.*) Guard! (*Guard.*) The daily report.

GUARD: Upstairs, a dog ran by.

HITLER: You hear that, Joseph. They are disguising themselves. They won't dare anymore to confront us openly. But I see through their tricks. I see through everything. A dog. Laughable! Continue.

GUARD: He pissed in the grass. That's all, my Führer.

HITLER: Keep your eyes open. The enemy is everywhere.

GUARD: Yessir, my Führer. (*Exit Guard.*)

HITLER: I'll address my people now. My people. (*Goebbels grabs his belly, screams, rolls screaming on the floor.*) A German mother doesn't scream. Guard! (*Guard.*) The midwife should be called. It's time. (*Exit Guard.*) That are the labor pains. Labor has started. I know that from my first marriage. (*Goebbels behaves hysterically.*) Are you still jealous of good old Ernst? Yes, he was a traitor. Even he. Do you remember how he looked at me when he saw my revolver. That wasn't what he expected. The little slut. How his jowls quivered. He had gotten a bit fat in those last days. I emptied the whole magazine into him. My hand didn't tremble. You were holding him, do you remember. You and Herrmann. Another traitor. I'm surrounded with traitors. My back is one big scar. All those stabs. Everywhere they are lying in wait for me. There. And there. (*Walks faster and faster back and forth, always whirling around suddenly.*) They are behind me. They won't dare to confront me. They are keeping themselves in my back. You see. But I'll get all of them. Providence is protecting me. (*Guard.*)

GUARD: The dog ran by again. He pissed again. The midwife.

(*Germania, enormous, with a midwife's bag.*)

GERMANIA: (*Hits Hitler in the belly, shakes his teeth, etc.*) How are you doing, my boy? Are you drinking your gasoline? Eating your men? Good. (*Grabs him by the testicles.*)

HITLER: (*Coyly.*) Mama!

GERMANIA: Still your Oedipus complex? (*Laughs.*)

HITLER: That's a Jewish obscenity.

GERMANIA: I won't have any more of that. I've had enough trouble with your Jewish nonsense. There are people who are pointing fingers at me. Even today. Some won't even say hello.

HITLER: The Jew . . .

(*Germania slaps his face. Hitler bawls.*)

GERMANIA: The pelvis is too tight. We'll have to use the forceps. Don't worry, it isn't my first time. But we aren't there yet. No reward without sweat. Open your legs. Breathe hard. And press. That's it. And a one, and a two. (*Guard.*)

GUARD: The three Magi of the Occident.

HITLER: You hear that, Joseph. We are attracting attention again. We are somebody again. The world . . .

GOEBBELS: DO YOU WANT TOTAL . . .

GERMANIA: Shut up.

HITLER: (*To the Guard.*) The Guard of Honor!

GERMANIA: (*To Goebbels.*) You could put on some rouge.

HITLER: A German mother . . .

GERMANIA: I've got to keep up with the times if I want to be in business again. (*Makes Goebbels up like a hooker.*) That'll do. (*To Hitler.*) And no goofing, you hear. Do the men know their lines?

HITLER: Providence . . .

GERMANIA: I'd rather like to be sure. (*The Guard of Honor. Dog heads, white crepe on black uniforms, bloodied boots, angel wings, they line up in formation.*) They could have polished their boots. Do I have to do everything myself. Pigs!

(*The three Magi review the Guard.*)

MAGI 1: Our seeds have grown.

MAGI 2: I don't like the boots.

MAGI 3: Veto. I don't like them either.

MAGI 1: We shouldn't forget what's at stake.

MAGI 2: Communism is a terrible threat.

MAGI 3: Especially to the soul.

MAGI 1: Just think of our children.

GUARD OF HONOR: (*Barks.*) FREEDOM DEMOCRACY THE WESTERN WORLD PEACE THERE'S NO PLACE LIKE HOME BETTER DEAD THAN RED ONLY A DEAD IN-DIAN IS A GOOD INDIAN TO EACH ONE HIS OWN UNI-TY IN PURITY

GERMANIA: (*With a sigh of relief.*) That worked nicely.

MAGI 1: What did I tell you.

MAGI 2: Indeed. A new spirit.

MAGI 3: Boots can be polished, after all.

GOEBBELS: (*Shouts.*) DO YOU WANT TOTAL . . .

HITLER: At this historical moment . . .

(*An enormous fart from Goebbels, spreading a foul smelling cloud, it topples the three Magi.*)

GUARD OF HONOR: Sieg Heil Sieg Heil Sieg Heil.

(*The three Magi shudder, hold their noses, get up.*)

GOEBBELS: My Führer.

GERMANIA: (*To Hitler.*) I hope it isn't just hot air. You never amounted to much in bed.

(*Hitler growls.*)

MAGI 3: It doesn't smell nice, does it.

MAGI 2: It indeed doesn't smell very nice.

MAGI 1: We shouldn't be petty.

MAGI 3: It's only natural, after all.

MAGI 2: It's human and not alien to me.

MAGI 3: Maybe, it's time now for our presents.

MAGI 2: We won't have to stay till the end.

MAGI 3: After all, everything is on track.

MAGI 1: The presents!

(*Soldiers of the three Magi bring the presents and exit.*)

MAGI 3: A set of torture tools. I've tried them myself. I believe, you have there a proverb. AS THE TWIG IS BENT . . .

MAGI 2: A historical toy for our dear little one. I grew up with it. Invigorates your self-confidence. Easy to operate. You put the cannon in position, load it, tie your man to the muzzle, and Bang! Comes with a set of colored people.

MAGI 1: Something for your kitchen. It's a fresh specimen. Only minimally damaged. From yesterday's hunt. We all have our little weaknesses.

HITLER: (*Grandly.*) I don't eat colored people.

MAGI 2: This fanaticism is embarrassing.

MAGI 3: Really, he isn't a person we should associate with.

MAGI 1: We musn't offend him. God knows when we'll need him again.

GERMANIA: (*To Hitler.*) We've got to keep up with the times. Even you. Won't you thank the gentlemen. (*Hitler growls and licks growling the shoes of the three Magi. Long scream from Goebbels.*) Gentlemen, it's time. Where's my forceps. Why don't you give me a hand. (*Germania applies the forceps, pulls, Magi 1 pulls at Germania, 2 at 1, 3 at 2.*)

HITLER: My people!

GUARD OF HONOR: GERMANY AWAKEN! SIEG HEIL!

THREE MAGIS: HALLELUJAH! HOSANNA! (*A wolf howls. Germania and the three Magi fall on their behinds. Before them rises a Thalidomide wolf. Startled.*) Oh.

(*Germania gets up, pulls a family-size box of SUNIL from her midwife's bag and pours detergent over the wolf. White light. The wolf is in sheep's clothing.*)

GERMANIA: (*To the three Magi.*) Did you say something? (*The wolf tears the black doll apart. Hitler tortures Germania who is held in place by the Guard of Honor. Goebbels dances like a whirling dervish. Germania screams.*)

HITLER: (*Laughs.*)

GUARD OF HONOR: GERMANY AWAKEN! SIEG HEIL!

GOEBBELS: (*Continues dancing.*)
OH HOW GOOD THAT NO ONE KNOWS

RUMPLESTILTSKIN IS MY NAME

WOLF: (*Howls.*)

THE THREE MAGI: (*Assuming the position of the three monkeys.*)
HALLELUJAH! HOSANNA!

(*Hitler loads the cannon. The Guard of Honor tie Germania to the muzzle. Curtain with the explosion.*)

THE WORKER'S MONUMENT
Building Site.

FOREMAN: The new guy. Government till yesterday. (*Exit.*)

FAT BRICKLAYER: The higher you climb . . .

NEW GUY: Better bricks than the clink

GENERAL: Here you can view your state from down below.

HILSE: General, promoted to the rank of worker.

GENERAL Your cross, Minister.

(*Heaves his backpack on the state-secretary's back. A white-collar worker puts up a streamer: WE'RE INCREASING OUR NORM.*)

YOUNG BRICKLAYER: Did you see that.

GENERAL: We'd love to work more, once again.

FAT BRICKLAYER: And for
   less money.

GENERAL: Not much longer.

YOUNG BRICKLAYER: You're the hero.

HILSE: (*To General.*) Is your brown hide itching.

GENERAL: Hail Stalin.

HILSE: I'll kill you.

GENERAL: I've learned how to do that, too.

(*The white-collar worker comes back and takes the streamer down.*)

HILSE: What's going on.

FAT BRICKLAYER: It's right face first and then
   Left face again.

WHITE-COLLAR WORKER: What do I know. I do
   As I'm told.

MINISTER: That's what they call the New Course.
   I was against it. I am for it now.

GENERAL: Shall I tell you what's going on. They are
Scared shitless.
FAT BRICKLAYER: Something's cooking, that's for sure.
HILSE: What does that mean: New Course.
MINISTER: Democracy.
The norm will be discussed before it's raised.
GENERAL: This isn't Russia. We aren't coolies.
FAT BRICKLAYER: Germans can take a lot. But not forever.
HILSE: You aren't paid for making speeches, General.
You too. There's work to do.
GENERAL: (*Makes a fist.*)   Do you remember
Thaelmann. IF OUR STRONG ARMS SHALL REFUSE . . .
HILSE: Do your work or else get off the site.

(*Factory whistles.*)

YOUNG BRICKLAYER: Somebody died again?
HILSE: What's going on?
GENERAL: Not yet, my boy.
FAT BRICKLAYER: (*To Hilse.*) You've got three guesses. Well?
VOICE: Colleagues, put your work down. We're on strike.
GENERAL: (*To Hilse.*) I've thought it over. I'll get off the site.
(*Throws his trowel down at Hilse's feet.*)
VOICE: Colleagues. Into the street. We're marching on
Government house.
GENERAL: We'll talk plain German now
To those comrades.
FAT BRICKLAYER: They understand only Russian.
(*Laughs about his joke.*)
GENERAL: They'll understand American alright.
HILSE: Hear RIAS speaking.
MINISTER: That's going too far.
GENERAL: (*To Hilse.*) Who's asking you, you Russki pet.
FAT BRICKLAYER: (*To Hilse.*)   The game
Is up, Franz.
GENERAL: Come on, if you aren't scabs. (*Exit.*)
FAT BRICKLAYER: Scared shitless?
YOUNG BRICKLAYER: (*To Hilse.*) Do you want to work alone.
HILSE: You won't drive me crazy.
FAT BRICKLAYER: What about you
Minister. Won't you join the working class?

I'll give you some advice: Who isn't for us
Is against us.
YOUNG BRICKLAYER: My first strike. A sailor
Should see it all. (*Leaves, holding his trowel.*)
HILSE: You know who you are joining.
YOUNG BRICKLAYER: Here, hold my trowel until I'm back. (*Hands him his trowel. Hilse is standing there, in each hand a trowel. Exit Young Bricklayer.*)
HILSE: You call yourself workers.
FAT BRICKLAYER: (*Laughs.*)   I?
MINISTER: The Russians
Are still here.
FAT BRICKLAYER: Yes. And the Americans. (*Exit.*)
MINISTER: I don't know if this will work, but surely
The old way didn't. (*Drops his backpack and exits.*)
HILSE: You won't drive me crazy.
(*Sorts out the broken bricks, replaces them, picks up the backpack.*)
Wasting the stuff. And that scum wants to strike.
(*Works. Teenagers, skinheads, with bicycles.*)
FIRST TEENAGER: Grandpa, did you put blinkers on your eyes?
No school today.
SECOND TEENAGER: He doesn't talk to us.
THIRD TEENAGER: Watch out, you'll get yourself a hernia, pop.
Piecework is murder.
FIRST: He has lost his marbles.
SECOND: Pop needs to make dough, Mom is crazy for a
Brand-new john.
THIRD: This way it's faster, grandpa.
(*Throws a brick at Hilse who is lugging bricks.*)
HILSE: Punk. Get off the building site.
SECOND: Grandpa
Is suicidal.
THIRD: That's the last alert.
Then it'll be live bullets. Drop it, pop.
FIRST: Join the people, or you'll be in trouble.
HILSE: What do you know, you snot.
FIRST: (*Angered, throws a brick.*)   Stupid old fart.
You're so sclerotic that your ears are clogged.

Man, he's so calcified you couldn't even
Boil him to make glue.
SECOND: Quick to the graveyard,
Pop, soon there won't be any place left. Your
Comrades are waiting at the gate in line.
HILSE: (*Furious.*) We've done for you . . . And you. You . . .
THIRD: (*Coldly.*)   I know some
Who are in jail today. But not tomorrow.
FIRST: Grandpa is blushing. Grandpa is ashamed.
SECOND: Grandpa is always blushing. Grandpa's red
Right to the marrow.
FIRST: (*Quickly.*)   Well, let's see. (*Throws a brick.*)
SECOND: Missed him.
FIRST: And this. And this. (*Throws and keeps hitting. The Old
Bricklayer is bleeding.*)
SECOND: You see, I've told you so.
FIRST: Right to the marrow. (*A sudden idea.*)
Can you dance, Grandpa? (*Improvises a rock tune, throws in time
with the beat. The others pick up the tune. All three are throwing
bricks at the Bricklayer, in time with the rock beat.*)
ALL THREE: Yea—
SECOND: Gotta jump
ALL THREE: Yea—
THIRD: You are learning, pop.
FIRST: And faster, pop.
SECOND: Don't fall asleep, pop.
THIRD: Hey.
You won't collapse on us.
SECOND: Pop's doing fine.
THIRD: Pop is doing great.
FIRST: Pop is tops
At the Marathon.
SECOND: Pop is the greatest.
(*A hail of bricks and the final flourish. The Bricklayer collapses
on the ground.*)
Looks like a workers' monument.
FIRST: (*Walks up to the Bricklayer.*)   Shit, man.
The guy is gone.
SECOND: Did you see anything?

THIRD: A workplace accident.

SECOND: Piecework is murder.

(The Three exit quickly.)

THE BROTHERS 1

There was nothing now to separate the Romans from the Cheruscans but the waters of the Weser. Arminius took his stand upon the further bank with his chiefs around him and inquired if Caesar had arrived. On being informed that he was there, he craved permission to speak with his brother Flavus, a man of noted loyalty, who had lost an eye while fighting under Tiberius some years before, and was now serving in the Roman army. Permission having been granted, Flavus stepped forward and was saluted by his brother. Dismissing his own attendants, Arminius requested that the bowmen posted on our side of the bank might be withdrawn. As soon as they had retired, he asked his brother how he had got that ugly wound upon his face. Informed of the place and occasion of the battle, Arminius inquired, what reward had he got for it? Flavus enumerated his increase of pay, his necklace and crown, and other military distinctions. Arminius scoffed at all these as the trumpery rewards of slavery.

Then began a colloquy in opposing strains. The one dwelt on the power of Rome, the wealth of Caesar, the heavy punishments meted to the conquered, the kindly treatment in store for his brother if he submitted: even his child and wife had not been treated as enemies. The other spoke of the sacred claims of country, of their ancestral freedom, of the national Gods of Germany, of their mother who added her prayers to his: let not Flavus choose to be the deserter and betrayer, rather than the leader, of his own kindred and his country. By degrees they fell to reproaches; and not even the intervening river would have kept them from coming to blows, had not Stertinius run up and held back Flavus, who was full of wrath, and crying out for horse and arms. On the other side Arminius was to be seen, threatening and challenging to combat: he used the Latin tongue freely in his discourse, having once commanded a force of his countrymen in our army.

Tacitus, *Annals* 0016
(Translation: G. G. Ramsay)

THE BROTHERS 2
Prison

GUARD: Step in the living room. Quite comfortable
  A toilet and so forth. (*Points at cell window:*)
                     And television
  Has been installed. If you don't like the channel
  Make a request and we'll take care of it.
SABOTEUR: Today we like it.
GUARD: Did you say something?
SABOTEUR: Why did they cancel our walk today.
GUARD: You could have caught a cold. The barometer
  Is quite unsteady since last night. Take this.
  (*Puts a pack of cigarettes into the newcomer's pocket. Exit.*)
SABOTEUR: His asshole's frozen shitless.
NEWCOMER: (*Looks at the cigarettes.*) What's going on
  Outside.
GHANDI: Let's have the cigarettes. (*Ghandi hands out the*
  cigarettes. Skips the Nazi.)
NEWCOMER: And he?
GHANDI: The Nazi doesn't smoke.
SABOTEUR: Why are you here?
GHANDI: He's political.
SABOTEUR: (*To the Newcomer.*) Sozi?
GHANDI: Communist.
SABOTEUR: Did you discover some hair in your stew?
  From a mustache? Or was it a goatee? (*Silence.*)
GHANDI: Why did you ask what's going on outside.
COMMUNIST: I'd like to know.
GHANDI: You're in the clouds.
COMMUNIST: How so?
GHANDI: You ask too many questions. We don't like that.
SABOTEUR: You'd like to see the stars?
NAZI: (*Steps forward.*)   He is my brother.
SABOTEUR: The Red?
GHANDI: (*Laughs.*) IN MY HOMETOWN IN MY HOMETOWN
  THAT'S WHERE WE MEET AGAIN.
COMMUNIST: My brother Snitch. (*Silence.*)
  You've made quite a career.
NAZI: And so did you.

(Pause. Noise of a crowd outside. Rhythmic beating on steam pipes in the prison that continues throughout the following scene.)

SABOTEUR: *(At the window.)* It won't take long now anymore.
COMMUNIST: *(At window.)*   What's that?
SABOTEUR: That is the people rising up.
COMMUNIST: They're drunk.
SABOTEUR: Say that again, you red dog.
COMMUNIST: From free beer.

(The Saboteur strikes the Communist down.)

NAZI: That guy has blown up bridges. Sabotage.
  He's working class. Could tell you tales about
  The underbelly of your paradise.
SABOTEUR: When I'm at last out of this place I won't
  Dirty my hands no more. Then I'll do better.

(The Communist tries to strike down the Saboteur. Ghandi steps in front of him.)

NAZI: And this is Ghandi. Got a life term. Murder.
  Ghandi works always with the knife. I'm sorry
  He hasn't got his knife with him. Tomorrow
  He'll have it back. It is a new beginning.
  The night of the long knives. Do you remember.
  I stood at your door. And I was your brother.
  (Holds out his hand. The brother doesn't take it.)
  My brother's hand wasn't available.
  I am your brother.
COMMUNIST: I don't have a brother.
NAZI: Better switch off the light, brother. The Reichstag
  Is burning bright enough. This is the night
  Of the long knives.
COMMUNIST: What do the bloodhounds get?
  Why don't you do your job. You'll get my bones
  After your butchers are finished with me.
  Where are they. Didn't you bring them along.
NAZI: I've brought them with me. Would you like to see them.
  They're here.
  (Takes off his jacket, shows his back, covered with old scars.)
          You know their signature. It is
  Still legible. It had become quite faded

In twenty years. But your friends came along
And they restored it. Old things are made new
So that my brother has something to read
On the vacation they've prescribed for him
So he'll recover from their Communism.
(*Ghandi and the Saboteur laugh.*)
COMMUNIST: We don't beat up people.
NAZI: Who is we?
(*Nazi, Ghandi, and the Saboteur laugh.*)
Do you recall how one becomes a snitch.
The brief instruction at Gestapo basement.
It seemed long to me. You're better off
Monday a Communist, Tuesday no longer
Because the Party said you never were one.
Three weeks long I received their special treatment
I did spit blood but not one syllable.
Then the discharge. Then back into the basement.
My flesh was torn to shreds, but not one name.
Released, nobody knew me anymore.
One time arrested and a snitch I was.
Who knew that they could never make me sing.
And when I went again into the basement
Backed up by nothing but my own torn back
I walked alone, for you I was The Snitch.
When I came out, it was The Snitch who had
Returned, he carried on his back his corpse
That carried other corpses on its back
Mangled like mine, and I had mangled them.
COMMUNIST: Why don't you put your jacket back on, snitch.
SABOTEUR: Why don't I teach the Red whose move it is now?
NAZI: He'll learn it soon enough when we are free.

(*Noise of crowd louder. A hodgepodge of words like: FREEDOM
GERMAN KILL THEM HANG THEM.*)

COMMUNIST: Why don't they shoot at them. This can't be true.
(*Hammers against the door.*)
Comrades, defend the prison. Shoot now, shoot.
GHANDI: Are my eyes seeing this. I don't believe it.
You'd like to serve your time, you idiot?
NAZI: Your comrades scurried into hiding, brother.

SABOTEUR: Don't worry, we'll find them all. And then
    We'll run them up the flagpole. Fly the banner!
    There will be room today at every flagstaff.
NAZI: (*To his brother.*) We'll hoist you only at half-mast.
COMMUNIST: Why don't I
    Have now the pistol which I didn't use
    To shoot you down, twenty years ago.
    Could I turn back the time . . .
GHANDI: Take the knife.
    The hands will also do. But that will need
    Some exercise. I'll teach you if you like.
    (*Closes his hands around his neck.*)
NAZI: It's too late for remorse. You're dying only
    Once. And I have done it. I have died.
    When I turned from your door that night of the
    Long knives and out of your hand dropped
    The revolver on the hallway floor
    Louder than any shot I've ever heard
    Before or after, and the bullet for
    The snitch your brother begged for on his knees
    Stayed in the barrel.
COMMUNIST: I'll beat you to a pulp.
NAZI: Beating to pulp, that was my specialty.
    Men, women, children, at Orel in Russia.
COMMUNIST: I didn't want to dirty my clean hands.
NAZI: And now there's blood on it. That's how the world turns.
Don't worry, brother, it's a slaughterhouse.
If you'd like to see what's got a future
Go to a factory where they make coffins.
You want to know your Socialism's face
Where hearts beat free in everybody's breast?
SABOTEUR: Because they've nothing on their ribs but skin.
COMMUNIST: You swine. You dirty swine.
GHANDI: Better be careful
    You're a minority in here, Comrade.
NAZI: I hope they make it till the Russians move.
SABOTEUR: So what. The Amis won't let us go under.
GHANDI: Against the Germans, they're all in cahoots.
SABOTEUR: They'll be surprised what Germans can pull off.

COMMUNIST: Maybe you won't be here to see it happen.
SABOTEUR: You scum. You traitor. Stupid Russian stooge.
COMMUNIST: You know, I've heard that once before, my friend.
    We were on transport on the Rennsteig highway
    From one camp to another concentration
    Camp, in trucks, Storm Troopers our guards,
    Handcuffed we traveled through the fatherland.
    It was in springtime. All the German birds were
    On active duty, and the German forest
    As green as only German trees are, only
    The wind was without fatherland, and we.
    Our guards were thirsty, had the transport stop
    At every second pub, filled up with beer
    Then took a leak, then guzzled beer again.
    For us they had a wonderful idea.
    At every stop they showed us to the people
    So they could spit at us. See the triators!
    They want to rob the German mother of
    Her child, the German husband of his wife.
    And so forth from their hymn book. And they came
    Babies in bellies, babies on their arms,
    And spit their venom into our face.
    We couldn't wipe it off, being handcuffed.
    They made us kneel in front of every child,
    I couldn't see with all the German spittle,
    The German country's beauty any longer.
    (*Ghandi and the Saboteur laugh.*)
    I closed my eyes and I saw more, much more.
    I saw the German birds flying in squadrons
    And shitting on the German forest green.
    Their shit exploded as they flew away
    And turned the green into an ashen black.
    The German children crawled from bloated bellies
    Of German mothers and ripped with their teeth
    The German pricks from their German fathers
    And pissed singing on the bleeding wound.
    And then they grabbed and bit their mothers' tits
    And drank their blood until the breasts turned barren,
    And then they tore into each other, screaming.

At last, they drowned in their own blood because
The German soil couldn't contain it all.
NAZI: Still singing the old psalm. What do you see now.

(Spits in his face. Noise of crowd decreases and is quickly fading in the distance. Noise of moving tanks. The beating on steam pipes stops.)

SABOTEUR: Did you hear that.
NAZI: Dammit.
GHANDI: What is that.
COMMUNIST: That is the tanks. The game is up and done with.
    And you will stay where you belong.
NAZI: With you.
    You like to hear the International
    When wheels of tanks are singing it, do you.
COMMUNIST: I never liked it better than today
    As it is sung by wheels of tanks, you snitch.
SABOTEUR: And soon you're going to hear angels singing.
    One of them should at least get it today.
GHANDI: He doesn't want it any different. He won't
    See Communism anyway.
COMMUNIST: Who am I.

(The three attack him.)

NIGHT PIECE

A man stands on stage. He is larger than life, maybe a dummy. He is dressed with posters. His face is without a mouth. He looks at his hands, moves the arms, tries moving his legs. A bicycle—its handlebars or pedals, or both, or handlebars, pedals, and saddle, have been removed—rolls quickly from right to left across the stage. The man, who may be a dummy, runs after the bicycle. A threshhold rises from the stage floor. He trips over it and falls down. Prostrate on his belly, he sees the bicycle vanish. The threshold disappears, unnoticed by him. When he gets up and looks for the cause of his fall, the stage floor is flat again. His suspicion falls on his legs. He tries to tear them off, sitting, on his back, standing. His heel against his buttocks, grabbing the foot with both hands, he tears off his left leg, then, flat on his face and prostrate, the right one. He is still lying on his belly when the bicycle slowly rolls by, from left to right across the stage. He notices it too late and, crawling, can't catch up with it. Raising himself and supporting his wavering trunk with his hands, he discovers that he can use his arms for locomotion if he sets his trunk into a swinging movement, throws it forward, then brings his hands forward, and so forth. He rehearses the new way of walking. He waits for the bicycle, first stage left, then stage right, at the proscenium. The bicycle doesn't appear. The man, who may be a dummy, tears the right with his left, and the left with his right hand, both arms off at the same time. Behind him the threshold rises from the stage floor to the level of his head, this time so that he won't fall. From the flies, the bicycle is lowered and comes to rest before him. Leaning against the threshold that is level with his head, the man, who may be a dummy, looks at his legs and arms, which lie scattered all over the stage, and at the bicycle that he won't be able to use anymore. He weeps one tear with each eye. Two Beckett-Spikes are moved in at eye level from both sides. They stop at the face of the man, who may be a dummy, he needs only to turn his head, once to the right, once to the left, the spike takes care of the rest. The spikes are moved off again, on the tip of each one an eye. From the empty eye sockets of the man, who may be a dummy, lice crawl and spread black all over his face. He screams. The mouth appears with his scream.

DEATH IN BERLIN 1

A pauper's graveyard rises, black, stones in line.
The dead look at the red ending of all
From their hole. It tastes like potent wine.
They sit, knitting, lined up against the wall
Caps of soot for naked skulls, and chime
The Marseillaise, the old battle call.

(Georg Heym)

DEATH IN BERLIN 2
Cancer Ward. Hilse. The Young Bricklayer.

YOUNG BRICKLAYER: How are you, Old Man.
HILSE: Since you ask me,
  I am not well. But I'm only one half
  Of me, the cancer ate the other half.
  And if you ask my cancer, he is fine.
YOUNG BRICKLAYER: I didn't know that. I was thinking
  It was the bricks they had piled on your bones
  At our building site two weeks ago
  Because you didn't want to strike.
HILSE: That's what I thought, too. I know better now.
  Once you permit those white coats just to touch you
  They'll find something. They won't spare anyone.
YOUNG BRICKLAYER: Shit on cancer. It will stop again.
HILSE: You are no doctor. You don't need to lie.
  We're of the same party, I and my cancer.
  This hand won't hold a trowel anymore.
  My last beer's stinking at the sewage plant.
  Shall I tell you what I would like once more.
  It is the only thing in this world, man
  You'll never get enough of. Word of honor.
  You can believe me. I've seen it all.
YOUNG BRICKLAYER: Yes. What shall I do. She's a whore, you
    know.
  And once I thought she was the Holy Virgin.
  And bragged about her like an idiot
  And no one told me anything, and all
  Of you knew it, yes, even you, and laughed
  Behind my back about the idiot
  Who picked himself a whore, right from the gutter
  And introduced her as the Holy Virgin.
  Did you all put your thing into her cunt.
  Do you know what sort of feeling that is,
  You're walking with an angel through Berlin
  You think she is an angel, beautiful
  As nobody you've ever had before—and I
  Can't count them on my fingers but like her

Was no one—if you see her legs, for instance,
You're feeling drunk immediately, and now
You're walking through Berlin with her and all
The guys who've got a cock are ogling her
And you think each one who gives her the eye
Has maybe once stuffed his one into her.
If someone, for example, told you that
Your party you have toiled and suffered for
And put up with your suffering since you knew
What's right and what is left, and now they tell you
She won't look any longer like herself
Your party, that much scum is on her hands
You'll climb the walls, won't need an elevator.
INTO MY ARMS YOU FLOWER OF THE GUTTER
She told me yesterday. She's told me all.
Since last night I didn't know how long
A night could last. And now the crazy part:
It's just the way it was before. I'm drunk
The moment I catch sight of her. INTO
MY ARMS YOU FLOWER OF THE GUTTER. Only
Once in a while, between my ribs, a knife
Is slowly twisted.
INTO MY ARMS YOU FLOWER OF THE GUTTER
I asked if she could lay a pipeline then
WATER FOR CANITOGA prick to prick.
Don't ask me why. Do you know what she said.
''I didn't count them.''—What shall I do now.
She is with child. She says it's mine.
HILSE: Did you bring her along.
YOUNG BRICKLAYER: She's waiting outside.

(*Exit. Sound of heartbeat. The dying begins. The Young Bricklayer comes back with the Girl.*)

HILSE: Red Rosa. Who'd have thought we'd meet again.
    Has the Spree River washed your blood off now.
    You're looking pale. Did they give you a hard time
    The rats of the Landwehr Canal. Those dogs
    Those yellow dogs. They sure are much worse than
    The rats. And I shall bet with anyone

That you liked being in the sewage from
Sweatshops—where they all knew you—better than
At the EDEN. That's their paradise.
The paradise of profiteers and butchers.
GIRL: What's he talking about.
YOUNG BRICKLAYER: I'll tell you later.
HILSE: The water didn't keep you, did it, Rosa.
   And even if they cook us all to soap
   It wouldn't wash their hands clean of your blood.
   Was it cold in the morgue. Do you know, Comrade
   That I had never seen you real close
   I mean like now, until that January
   When, your eyes blinded, you lay on that bier.
   We were filing by you for twelve hours
   Then through Berlin we marched behind your coffins
   No word was spoken and the sky was lead.
   Now you are looking younger. (*Slyly.*) I know why.
   I'm the eternal bricklayer, you know me?
   The pyramids in Egypt, that old fortress
   Against all time, they are my handwriting.
   And I've built Rome, on its seven hills
   Anew after each fire and each war.
   The Capitol, for instance, and the column
   Where Caesar bled himself to death, between
   His ribs the daggers, twenty three of them.
   And then the skyscrapers of New York City.
   And it was always for the capitalists
   Ten Thousand years and longer. But in Moscow
   The first time ever I was my own boss:
   The subway. Have you seen it. And at last
   I have immured the capitalists. One brick
   One trowel mortar. If you still had eyes
   You could see them, shining through my hands
   The red banners over Rhine and Ruhr.
YOUNG BRICKLAYER: You should say something now. Anything.
GIRL: I can see them without eyes
   (*The Young Bricklayer prompts her.*)
                       Comrade
The red banners—

(*The Young Bricklayer prompts.*)
                                  Over Rhine and Ruhr.
(*The dying Bricklayer smiles.*)
HILSE: Is Friedrichsfelde Cemetery too quiet
  For you.
GIRL: No. Sometimes we hear children playing
  They're playing Bricklayer and Capitalist.
HILSE: (*Laughs.*) And no one wants to be Capitalist.
GIRL: Yes.

(*Sound of heartbeat stops. Silence.*)

1956/71

MÜLHEIM ADDRESS

MÜLHEIM ADDRESS (Mülheimer Rede) was written when Heiner Müller received for GERMANIA TOD IN BERLIN the Mülheim Dramatists Prize 1979, the prestigious West German prize for new drama. He had been invited to give the key address at the "Mülheim Days of Theatre" in September of the same year but was unable to attend.

The text defines Müller's political and aesthetic position at the time and his views of West German drama and theatre.

C. W.

Honorable Mr. Mayor, Ladies and Gentlemen:

I regret that I am not able to participate in this event, the more so since this year one of my works represents its cause. Rehearsal for the première of an older play of mine is in a phase that demands my participation in a more than usually required manner, besides I have started work on a new piece. In this situation my appearance in Mülheim would cost me more than just two work days. I therefore ask you to understand my decision to decline the invitation.

The desire to hear me speak about today's dramatic literature causes me some embarrassment. The reality of drama, the theatre, is always the present and in our present situation HAMLET concerns me more than GODOT, WALLENSTEIN more than MOTHER COURAGE, to name examples of approximately equal rank. I am talking about plays, not about authors. Still, and always again, Brecht's FATZER fragment interests me more than Shakespeare's WINTER'S TALE. That the classic works still have an impact results from their store of utopia; that they can't be written any longer, or not yet again, from the fact that utopia is endangered, that is, has disappeared. The topic of recent drama is the ALREADY or the STILL, a question of the political standard: Man diminished. Many of the best brains and gigantic industries are busily working at the disappearance of Man. Consumption is the practice drill of the masses in this process, each item of merchandise a weapon, every supermarket a boot camp. This demonstrates the necessity of art as a means of making reality impossible. The gravity of the masses, in Capitalism the condition, is in a Socialist society the corrective of politics, the blindness of experience is proof of its authenticity. Socialism—clichés of dissidence and/or dogma won't capture reality: it doesn't dwell in extremes. That which is history to the elites has always been labor to the masses. Clichés satisfy the appetite for signals of treason from the camp on the other side of Capitalism, they guarantee the good conscience of consumption, the peace of corruption. Only the increasing pressure of authentic experience will develop the capacity to see into the white of history's eye. The SpaceTime of art is between the time of the subject and that of history, the difference a potential theatre of operations. My difficulty in dealing with the dramatic literature from your other German state is rooted in my post-bourgeois experience with another subject and another history. Black drama in the USA is less alien to me than the

Capitalistic tragedies of Botho Strauss where history only appears by its absence, as a void, that is, as the movement of capital hidden to view, the fear of losing your status as a religious experience. Thomas Bernhard's gray-black farces which recently have been traded as dynamism by sensitive critics who imbue them with their own private sorrows, remain fiercely affirmative jokes as long as the theatre's market constraints exorcise the sadness from these texts. My solidarity belongs to Franz Xaver Kroetz and his heroic effort to assert in the political vacuum that is the center of your world Communism as a middle position, though my own experience views it rather as the Other. In both German states drama is a much larger field than the theatres are ready or able to traverse; the more so we should appreciate an institution like the Mülheim Days of Theatre which at least makes the illusion possible that there is also in the Federal Republic a widespread interest in today's production of German-language drama. Altogether, playwriting is a lonesome business again, and the theories have turned gray in the idle chatter of discussions; this can only be changed by politics and not without art's contribution to politics.

Since FATZER'S WALKS THROUGH THE CITY OF MÜLHEIM which reflects in angry sentences the connection between war and business, little probably has changed in the property conditions of Mülheim. In this respect, the Prize for Dramatists is something like a letter of indulgence. My hope is a world where plays like GERMANIA DEATH IN BERLIN could no longer be written because reality no longer offered their subject matter. With this in mind I thank the city of Mülheim for its prize.

Heiner Müller, September 6, 1979

Explosion of a Memory /
Description of a Picture

EXPLOSION OF A MEMORY / DESCRIPTION OF A PICTURE
(*Bildbeschreibung*) was written in 1984 and first published in Rotbuch # 290, *Shakespeare Factory 1*, volume 8 of *Heiner Müller
Texte*, West Berlin, 1985, and also by Droschl Verlag, Graz, 1985,
on the occasion of its first performance during the Austrian theatre
festival "Steirischer Herbst," at Vereinigte Bühnen, Graz, October
6, 1985, in a production directed by Gina Cholakova. Müller had
earlier offered the text to Robert Wilson when the director asked him
for a prologue to his *Alcestis* project, to be staged first at American
Repertory Theatre in Cambridge, Mass., and later at Staatstheater,
Stuttgart. These productions occurred in 1986 and 1987. A first
version of this translation for the Cambridge performance was
published in *Performing Arts Journal* 28, New York, 1986.

The piece had been evoked in Müller's mind by the drawing of a
young Bulgarian student which he was given in the late sixties. In an
interview, published in PAJ 28, Müller stated: "She had a dream
and she was drawing the dream. I was interested in this drawing
because it was not a work of art. She never read one line of Freud
and doesn't know anything about it, but it had a very clear and very
compelling psychoanalytic surface." He began to jot down notes
about the drawing in the early seventies, but actually wrote the piece
nearly fifteen years later. Such long germination of an idea is quite
usual for Müller's work. In this context, it is interesting that he
eventually wrote portions of the text in an act of "automatic
writing," very much like the process the surrealists proposed. Quite
logically, he wanted a quote from his end note, "Explosion of a
Memory," to be used for the English title.

Müller claims this note, with its citing of Hitchcock's *The Birds*,
was mainly written to mislead future directors: "I like to confuse
them. A danger . . . is that the director has a clear concept and then
he breaks the text . . . and kills the play with his concept." However
that may be, the sources mentioned in the note can clearly be traced
in the text; in particular, Homer's Eleventh Canto of the *Odyssey*

provided themes and imagery to it. The piece continues Müller's thirty-five-year-long revisioning of the classic Greco-Roman tradition of Western culture, as it is documented by other texts in this volume, HAMLETMACHINE, and THE BATTLE.

The translation's use of punctuation may at times differ from familiar usage to the same extent as the German original does. Michael Roloff collaborated on this second English version.

C. W.

EXPLOSION OF A MEMORY (Description of a Picture)
as prologue to *Alcestis*
Director: Robert Wilson
American Repertory Theatre, Cambridge, Mass., 1986

DESCRIPTION OF A PICTURE
Vereinigte Bühnen Krefeld/Mönchengladbach, 1985

A landscape neither quite steppe nor savannah, the sky a Prussian blue, two colossal clouds float in it as though held together by wires, or some other structure that can't be determined, the larger one on the left might be an inflated rubber animal from an amusement park that has broken away from its mooring, or a chunk of Antarctica flying home, at the horizon a low mountain range, to the right—in the landscape—a tree, upon closer inspection there are three trees, each a different size, mushroom shaped, trunk next to trunk, perhaps with the same root, the house in the foreground a prefab rather than the work of craftsmen, probably of concrete: a window, a door, the roof hidden by the leaves of the tree that stands in front of the house, overgrowing it, a tree of a different species than the clump in the background, its fruits apparently edible, or fit for poisoning guests, a glass bowl on a garden table, still partially shaded by the treetop, contains six or seven available specimens of the citrus-like fruit, from the position of the table, a crude handhewn piece, the crosslegs made of unfinished young birch trunks, one may conclude that the sun or whatever it is that sheds light on this place stands at its Zenith at this instant of the picture, perhaps THE SUN is always there and TO ETERNITY: that it moves can't be verified from the picture, the clouds too, if clouds they are, are floating perhaps at one and the same spot, the wiring their attachment to a blotchy blue board with the whimsical designation SKY, a bird on a branch, the leaves concealing its identity, a vulture or a peacock or a vulture with a peacock's head, gaze and beak pointed at a woman whose image rules the right half of the picture, her head splitting the mountain range in two, the face is gentle, very young, the nose too long, with a swelling at its root, perhaps a fist hit her, her gaze directed on the ground as though there were an image she cannot forget and/or another one she refuses to see, her hair long and wispy, blond or whitish-gray, the harsh light makes no distinction, her clothing a moth-eaten fur coat, tailored for broader shoulders, flung over a threadbare flimsy shirt, likely of linen, from whose right sleeve, too wide and badly frayed at one spot, a fragile forearm lifts a hand to heart level, i.e., the left breast, a defensive gesture or from the language of deaf-mutes, the defense is meant against a familiar terror, the blow shove stab has happened, the shot has been fired, the wound no longer bleeds, the repetition hits a void where there is no room left for fear, the woman's face becomes readable if the second assumption is right, a rat's face, an angel of the rodents, the jaws grinding word carcasses and language debris, the left coat sleeve hanging in tatters as after an accident or an assault by some fanged beast or machine, peculiar that the arm isn't injured, or are the brown stains on the sleeve dried blood, the gesture of the long-fingered right hand, is it meant for a pain in the left shoulder, is the arm hanging limply in its sleeve broken or disabled by a flesh wound, the arm is cropped at the wrist by the picture's edge, the hand might be a claw, a stump (encrusted with blood perhaps) or a hook, up to even above her knees the woman stands in a void, amputated by the picture's edge, or is she growing from the ground as the man steps from the house and will disappear into the ground again as the man into the house, until one unending movement sets in which bursts the frame, the flight, the tree root engine pouring lumps of earth and ground water, visible only between one glimpse and the next when the eye HAVING SEEN IT ALL squinting closes over the picture, between tree and woman wide open the large solitary window, the curtain billows out, the storm appears to issue from inside the house, no hint of wind in the tree, or is the woman attracting the storm, or does her appearance evoke it in the ashes of the fireplace where the storm has been waiting for her, what or who has been burned, a child, another woman, a lover, or are the ashes her actual remains, her body on loan from the graveyard's stockpile, the man in the doorway, his right foot on the brown patchy grass that is parched by an unknown sun, holds in his right hand, arm extended, with a hunter's grip a bird at the spot where you tear off the wing, the left hand, equipped with overlong curved fluttering fingers, caresses its feathers, ruffled by deathly fear, the bird's beak wide open to emit a shriek inaudible to the viewer, as it is dumb to the bird in the tree which isn't interested in birds, the skeleton of his kin, visible through the window rectangle at the black-veined interior wall which he cannot see from his place in the tree, would have no message for him, the man is smiling, his step is winged, a dance step, no way of telling if he's already seen the woman, perhaps he has lost his sight, his smile the blindman's precaution, he is seeing with his feet, every stone his foot stumbles on is laughing at him, or it's the smile of the murderer on his way to work, what is going to happen at the crosslegged table with the bowl full of fruit and the overturned shattered wine glass with the remains of a black liquid still swirling that spilled on the table top and is dripping down at the edge spreading in ever wider puddles on the ground under the table, the high-backed chair in front of which has its peculiarity: halfway up its four legs are tied by wire as if to keep the chair from collapsing, a second chair lies discarded behind a tree on the right, its back broken, the protective wiring merely a Z, not a rectangle, perhaps an early attempt at fastening, which strain broke the chair, made the other unstable, a murder perhaps, or violent copulation, or both at once, the man on the chair, the woman on top of him, his member in her vagina, the woman still heavy from the grave soil out of which she worked her way to visit the man, from the ground water with which her furcoat is dripping, her movement first a gentle rocking, then an increasingly vehement riding, until the orgasm thrusts the man's back against the back of the chair that gives way with a crack, the woman's back against the edge of the table top upsetting the wine glass, the bowl loaded with fruit starts to slide and when the woman throws herself forward, her arms clutching the man, his arms under the furcoat clutching her, he biting her neck, she biting his, it comes to a stop with the table just by its edge, or the woman on the chair, the man standing behind her, his hands placed around her neck, thumb to thumb, first like in a game, only the middle fingers touching, then, as the woman rears against the back of the chair, her fingernails clawing the muscles of his arms, the veins in her neck and her forehead protruding, her head filling with blood coloring the face a bluish red, her legs knock twitching against the table top, the wine glass topples, the bowl starts to slide, the strangler closes the circle, thumb to thumb, finger to finger, till the woman's hands drop off his arms and the soft cracking of the larnyx or the vertebrae indicates the work's finish, perhaps the back of the chair gives way again now under her weight as the man withdraws his hands, or the woman slumps forward with her bluish red face falling against the wine glass from which the dark liquid, wine or blood, seeks its way to the ground, or is the streaky shadow at the woman's neck beneath her chin a knife incision, the streaks dried blood from a wound as wide as the neck, black with clotted blood also the strands of hair to the right of her face, trace of the lefthanded murderer on the threshold, his knife writes from right to left, he'll need it again, it bulges under the cloth of his jacket, when the broken glass reassembles its shards and the woman steps to the table, no scar on her throat, or it will be the woman, the thirsty angel, who bites the bird's throat and pours its blood into the glass from the open neck, the food of the dead, the knife isn't meant for the bird, up to eye level the man's face is earthcolored, forehead and visible hand, the other hidden by the plumage of the bird he holds, is as white as paper, he seems to wear gloves when working outside, why not at the moment of the picture, and something like a hat against the hot star that shines down on the landscape bleaching its colors, what might his work be, apart from the perhaps daily murder of the perhaps daily resurrected woman, in this landscape, animals appear only as clouds, no hand can catch them, the bird in the tree is the last of its kind, one call and he is snared, no need to pull up the grass, the SUN, maybe a multitude of SUNS, will scorch it, the fruits of the bird-tree are quickly plucked, have the fluttering fingers of the strangler knitted the steel mesh round the low mountain range from which only one paper-white peak protrudes, still un-protected, the mesh protection against rock slides triggered by the wanderings of the dead, underground, the secret pulse of the planet which the picture is meant to represent, protection offering some prospect of permanence perhaps when the growth of the graveyards will have reached its limit with the small weight of the presumed murderer on the threshold, of the swiftly digested bird in the tree, there's space on the wall for its skeleton, or will the movement go into reverse when the number of the dead is complete, will the throng of graves turn into the tempest of resurrection that will drive the snakes out of the mountain, is the woman with the furtive gaze and the mouth like a suction cup a MATA HARI of the nether-world, reconnoiterer exploring the terrain where the Grand Maneuver shall be held that will wrap the starved bones in flesh, the flesh in skin, shot through with veins that drink blood from the ground, homecoming of the viscera from nothingness, or is it a hollow angel under her dress because the dwindling meat pit beneath the ground refuses to yield further bodies, an EVIL FINGER held up in the wind by the dead against the police of the heavens, harbinger and BRIDE OF THE WIND who steals the wind from the natural foes of the resurrection in the flesh, the wind which they inhabit, it blows, a storm, into the trap, the curtain's arrow points at the woman, the murderer, too, perhaps merely a corpse-on-duty, his (secret) mission the extermination of birds, the relaxed dance step signifying the imminent completion of his work, perhaps the woman already is on her way back into the ground, pregnant by the storm, seed of the rebirth from an explosion of corpses, bones, splinters, and marrow, the wind supply marking the distance between the parts, the parts which perhaps once, when after the resettlement of the air for breathing an earthquake blasts them through the planet's skin, THE WHOLE will reassemble, the star's insemination by its own dead, first signal the clouds with their wiring which actually is made of nerve fibers that precede the bones, i.e., of spiderwebs from the bone marrow, like the vine's tendrils without visible roots that are climbing the walls of the bungalow, already covering the inside as far as the ceiling, or the wire tangle of the chairs, or the steel mesh that nails the mountain range to the ground, or it's all different: the mesh the whim of a careless crayon that refused to provide plasticity to the mountains with its botched hatching, perhaps the composition's capriciousness adheres to a plan, the tree standing on a tray, its roots cut off, the oddly shaped trees in the background especially long stemmed mushrooms, plants of a climate that doesn't know trees, how did the slab of concrete appear in the landscape, no trace of transportation or vehicle, I TOLD YOU YOU SHOULDN'T COME BACK DEAD IS DEAD, no tracks of dragging or hauling, was it forced out of the ground, dropped from the SKY, or did the arm of a crane controlled from a fixed point in the above called SKY lower it out of air only the dead can breathe, is the mountain range a museum piece, on loan from a subterranean showroom where the mountains are stored because at their natural habitat they obstruct the low flights of angels, the "whole" picture an experimental set-up, its crude design an expression of contempt for the experimental animals man, bird, woman, the blood pump of the daily murder, man against bird and woman, woman against bird and man, bird against woman and man, provides fuel for the planet, blood the ink that inscribes its paper life with colors, even its sky threatened with anemia by the resurrection of the flesh, wanted: the gap in the process, the Other in the recurrence of the Same, the stammer in the speechless text, the hole in eternity, the possibly redeeming ERROR: the distracted gaze of the killer while he probes the throat of his victim on the chair with his hands, with the edge of the knife, at the bird in the tree, into the emptiness of the landscape, hesitating before the incision, a closing of the eyes before the gush of blood, the woman's laughter, one glimpse long loosening the stranglehold, making tremble the hand with the knife, the bird dive-bombing at the blade's gleam, the landing on the man's skull, the beak's slashes, one right, one left, reeling and roaring of the blinded, blood spraying in the tempest's whirl, who gropes for the woman, fear that the blunder will be made while he's squinting, that the peephole into Time will open between one glimpse and the next, hope lives on the edge of the knife that rotates ever faster, with increasing attention that equals fatigue, insecurity lightening the certainty of the ultimate horror: MURDER is an exchange of sexes, ALIEN IN YOUR OWN BODY, the knife is the wound, the neck is the axe, is the fallible surveillance part of the plan, to which instrument is the lens attached that leeches all color from the view, in which socket is the retina stretched, who OR WHAT inquires about the picture, TO LIVE IN A MIRROR, is the man doing the dance step: I, my grave his face, I: the woman with the wound at her throat, right and left in her hands the split bird, blood on the mouth, I: the bird who with the script of his beak shows the murderer the way into the night, I: the frozen storm.

DESCRIPTION OF A PICTURE may be read as an overpainting of Euripides' ALCESTIS which quotes the Noh play KUMASAKA, the Eleventh Canto of the ODYSSEY, and Hitchcock's THE BIRDS. The text describes a landscape beyond death. The action is optional since its consequences are past, explosion of a memory in an extinct dramatic structure.

H. M., 1985

THE WOUND WOYZECK

For Nelson Mandela

THE WOUND WOYZECK (Die Wunde Woyzeck) is a speech Müller read at Darmstadt, October 18, 1985, when he received the Georg Büchner Prize of the German Academy for Language and Poetry, West Germany's most important literary honor. It was published in *Theater Heute* #11, Berlin, 1988. Its first printing in English appeared in *Performing Arts Journal* 30 (Vol. X, No. 3), New York 1987, in this translation. Subsequently, it was published in the international collection of writings edited by Jacques Derrida, entitled *For Nelson Mandela* (Seaver Books, 1987).

Müller began with a reference to the execution of the black poet Benjamin Moloise at Central Prison of Pretoria the same morning, stating that it was a shock to see his prepared text so immediately corroborated by this political murder in South Africa.

The text is less an expression of thanks than a stream of associations, linking Büchner's anti-hero with writers such as Kafka, Kleist, Lenz, Heine, Georg Heym, Konrad Bayer, with figures of contemporary political struggles such as Ulrike Meinhof, and with a literary character, the Young Comrade in Brecht's play *The Measures Taken*.

Ending with an attack against the theory of so-called ''Post-Histoire,'' Müller refers to a German proverbial saying, ''Da liegt der Hund begraben'' (''That's where the dog is buried''), which means roughly: This is the root of the problem, the cause of it all.

C. W.

1   Woyzeck still is shaving his Captain, eating the prescribed peas, torturing Marie with the torpor of his love, the play's population has become a state, surrounded by ghosts: The Fusilier Runge is his bloody brother, proletarian tool of Rosa Luxemburg's murderers; his prison is called Stalingrad where the murdered woman faces him in the mask of Kriemhild; her monument is erected on Mamaia Hill, her German monument the Wall in Berlin, the armored train of the Revolution curdled to politics. HIS MOUTH PRESSED AGAINST THE SHOULDER OF THE POLICEMAN WHO NIMBLY LEADS HIM AWAY, that is how Kafka has seen him disappear from the stage, after the fratricide WITH DIFFICULTY STIFLING THE LAST NAUSEA. Or as the patient, in whose bed the doctor is placed, with his wound open like a mine pit from which the maggots swarm. Goya's giant was his first appearance, he who sitting on the mountains counts the hours of the rulers, father of the guerilla. On a mural in a cloister cell in Parma I have seen his broken off feet, gigantic in an Arcadian landscape. Somewhere, his body perhaps swings itself onward on his hands, shaking with laughter perhaps, toward an unknown future that perhaps will be his crossbreeding with a machine, propelled against the force of gravity in the frenzy of rockets. In Africa he is still on his Way of the Cross into history, time doesn't work for him any more, perhaps even his hunger isn't an ingredient of Revolution any longer since it can be quenched with bombs, while the Drum Majors of the world devastate our planet, a battlefield of Tourism, runway for the final emergency; they don't see the Fire that the Rifleman Franz Johann Christoph Woyzeck saw race around the sky near Darmstadt as he was cutting switches for the gauntlet. Ulrike Meinhof, a daughter of Prussia and late-born bride of another erratic block of German letters who buried himself on Wannsee shore, female protagonist in the last drama of a bourgeois world, the armed RESURRECTION OF THE YOUNG COMRADE FROM THE LIME PIT, she is his sister with Marie's bloody necklace.

2   A text many times raped by the theatre, a text that happened to a twenty-three-year-old whose eyelids were cut off at his birth by the Weird Sisters, a text blasted by fever to orthographic splinters, a structure as it might be created when lead is smelted at New Year's Eve since the hand is trembling with anticipation of the future; a

sleepless angel it blocks the entrance to Paradise where the in-
nocence of playwriting was at home. How harmless the Pill's
equivalent in recent drama, Beckett's WAITING FOR GODOT,
faced with this fast thunderstorm that moves with the speed of
another age, in its baggage Lenz, the extinguished lightning from
Livonia, the time of Georg Heym bereft of utopia in his space under
the Havel river's ice, of Konrad Bayer in Vitus Bering's eviscerated
skull, of Rolf Dieter Brinkmann in the right-hand traffic in front of
SHAKESPEARE'S PUB; how shameless the lie of POST-
HISTOIRE in the face of the barbaric reality of our own prehistory.

3   THE WOUND HEINE begins to scar over, crooked;
WOYZECK is the open wound. Woyzeck lives where the dog is
buried, the dog's name: Woyzeck. We are waiting for his resurrection with fear and/or hope that the dog will return as a wolf. The
wolf will come from the South. When the Sun is in its Zenith, he
will be one with our shadow and in the hour of white heat History
will begin. Not until History has happened will our shared destruction in the frost of entropy or, abridged by politics, in the nuclear
lightning, be worthwhile; the destruction which will be the end of all
utopias and the beginning of a reality beyond mankind.

1985

VOLOKOLAMSK HIGHWAY

VOLOKOLAMSK HIGHWAY (*Wolokolamsker Chausee*) is a cycle of performance texts which reflect the form of the "dramatic poem," a familiar genre in German classic literature of the late eighteenth and early nineteenth centuries.

Part 1, RUSSIAN GAMBIT (*Russische Eröffnung*), written in 1984, had its premiere May 8, 1985 (the fortieth anniversary of Germany's capitulation at the end of World War II) at the Deutsches Theater, East Berlin, in a production directed by Alexander Lang. It opened the same month at West Germany's Schauspielhaus Bochum, staged by Alfred Kirchner. First published in the East Berlin literary journal *Sinn und Form*, March/April 1985, and in the West Berlin theatre magazine *Theater Heute* #7, 1985, it appeared also in Rotbuch # 290, *Shakespeare Factory 1*, West Berlin, 1985.

The text follows quite closely an episode in Alexander Bek's book *Volokolamskoe Shosse*, which narrates the struggles of a Red Army infantry battalion during the Battle for Moscow, in October 1941, when invading Nazi armies threatened the Soviet capital. Bek's book also provided the title for the complete cycle.

Part 2, FOREST NEAR MOSCOW (*Wald bei Moskau*), also written in 1985, was first performed May 4, 1986, at Hans-Otto-Theater of Potsdam, in a production directed by Bernd Weissig. Again Müller based his play on Alexander Bek's work, though here a motif of the narrative was freely adapted.

Part 3, THE DUEL (*Das Duell*), written in 1986, also had its first production at Hans-Otto-Theater, Potsdam, staged by Weissig in March 1987. The text employs a motif from Anna Seghers, the author who earlier had provided the source for Müller's play THE TASK. The scene describes a contest of wills between a plant manager and his deputy on June 17, 1953, the day large numbers of East German workers rose up in protest against an enforced wage structure, and eventually against the imposed political system of the

GDR, until Russian troops quickly quelled the insurrection. The Potsdam performance was the first presentation of those 1953 events to appear on a GDR stage.

Note: "V. E. B. October" and "Progress" were names of nationalized plants.

"Goatee" was the nickname of Party Secretary Walter Ulbricht, the then most powerful politician in the GDR.

"Germany Above All Nations" (*Deutschland über Alles*) was Germany's national anthem until 1945.

"Workers and Farmers College" (*Arbeiter und Bauern Fakultät*): special colleges had been established in the late forties to prepare working class students without a high school education for university entrance.

"New Germany" (*Neues Deutschland*): the name of the official paper of the Socialist Unity Party (SED), the ruling party of the GDR; in context the term also attains a metaphoric meaning.

"Madrid You Beautiful" (*Madrid Du Wunderbare*): song of the German battalion of the International Brigades which fought with the Republican army during the Spanish Civil War.

T-34: the most common type of tank used at the time by the Soviet army.

Part 4, CENTAURS (*Kentauren*), also written in 1986, was first performed as an insert in Scene 14 of *The Scab*, in Müller's own production at the Deutsches Theater, East Berlin, January 1988. It was first published in *Theater der Zeit*, East Berlin, February 1988, and then in *Theater Heute* # 3, 1988.

The text describes a nightmare of the officer-in-charge at an East Berlin precinct of the "People's Police," as the East German police force is called. The sub-title refers to Gregor Samsa, the hero of Kafka's *Metamorphosis* who turns overnight into a giant cockroach. Neither Kafka nor Samsa were Saxonians, of course, but the dialect of many state officials and police officers in the GDR is Saxonian since about two-thirds of the population speak Saxonian or a related dialect. Many allusions in the text refer to East German history, habits, lingo, and so forth, and it requires an intimate knowledge of the GDR to fully appreciate the play's irony and humor.

Note: The German term for "red tape" is "*Amtsschimmel.*" It signifies the same idea as "red tape" while it means literally "ad-

ministrative mildew'' as well as ''administrative white horse''
(*Schimmel* = white horse, or mildew). The allusion of ''Centaur''
to ''White horse'' is, of course, lost in translation.

The quote from *The Tempest* is in English in the original.

''I Am a Man, a Man Who's Like an Oaktree'' is a paraphrase of
the first line of a song in praise of Ernst Thaelmann, leader of the
German Communist Party (KPD) during the twenties and thirties,
and killed in Buchenwald Concentration Camp in 1945. The song
compared Thaelmann to Rosa Luxemburg and Karl Liebknecht who
had been murdered by right wing Imperial Guard officers in
January 1919. The song was later appropriated by the Nazi movement, reworded in praise of Hitler.

''Knock wood'' is not quite an equivalent for the German ''*Gut
Holz*'' (Good Wood!) which is a bowling term.

''Clean ...'' stands for ''*Sau...,*'' the first syllable of
''*Sauberkeit*'' (cleanliness), while the word ''*Sau*'' means sow,
creating a pun on ''*Sau Bedienung!*'': ''The service stinks!''

Part 5, THE FOUNDLING (*Der Findling*), written in 1987, was
first presented as a reading by the author during a matinee performance, January 31, 1988, at the Deutsches Theater, East Berlin. It
was printed in *Theater Heute Yearbook '88*, Berlin, 1988.

Employing motifs from Heinrich von Kleist's short story *Der
Findling* (1811), the text explores the conflict between a former concentration camp inmate, who became a high-ranking official in the
Socialist Unity Party (SED) of East Germany—probably serving
with the military or the police force—and his adopted son whom he
found as a baby in the ruins of Berlin in 1945. In a monologue the
son recalls their shared past and the historical events which led to
their estrangement, a split that has become irrevocable. The piece
addresses itself to an audience thoroughly familiar with history and
societal developments of the GDR and other Socialist countries, an
audience which has experienced much of the past to which the narrative alludes.

Note: The City of Bautzen is the site of the GDR's best known
penitentiary where political convicts especially were detained; the
word ''Bautzen'' has become proverbial.

August 1968: forces of the Warsaw Pact states invaded
Czechoslovakia to put an end to the reforms the Communist Party,
under its leader Alexander Dubcek, had initiated there during the

so-called ''Prague Spring.''

Ploetzensee: the prison where the officers and other participants of the failed 1944 conspiracy against Hitler were hanged from meat hooks.

Landwehrkanal: a waterway in Berlin where, in 1919, the corpses of the leftist leaders Rosa Luxemburg and Karl Liebknecht were dumped by their murderers, officers of the Imperial Guards.

TO EACH HIS OWN and LABOR MAKES YOU FREE: inscriptions at the gate of several concentration camps.

''New Germany'': see above.

''Red Neckcloth'': worn by all members of the organization ''Young Pioneers'' which shares certain features with the Boy Scouts and is a branch of the FDJ.

''Blue Shirt'': worn by members of the ''Free German Youth'' (FDJ), the organization for young people of all ages.

Berlin Wall: erected in 1961 by the East German government to stop the increasing emigration from the GDR to West Germany. Many East Germans were shot while trying to cross this fortified state border in Berlin.

''Thaelmann Song,'' ''Partisans of the Amur,'' ''Onward to the Final Fight,'': songs every young person in the GDR learned and sang in school or the FDJ. The last quote is a line from the ''Internationale.''

Kronstadt: the port near St. Petersburg where an uprising of sailors of the Baltic Fleet was crushed by the Soviet government.

The completed cycle had its world première on February 23, 1988, at the Theatre de Bobigny, Paris, directed by Jean Jourdheuil and Jean-François Peyret in a translation by Jean-Pierre Morel, titled *La Route des Chars* (The Road of the Tanks); a first production in the original language opened on November 11, 1988 at the Cologne Schauspiel, in Manfed Karge's staging. The cycle was published, together with THE BATTLE, as a volume of *Theaterbibliothek*, (Verlag der Autoren, Frankfurt, 1988).

In his endnote Müller defines the cycle as his third experiment in writing a ''Proletarian tragedy'' in a post-revolutionary period or, in his own words, an ''age of counter-revolution,'' a tragedy whose protagonists are torn or destroyed by the dialectics of history as an ancient Prometheus or Oedipus were by fate.

With VOLOKOLAMSK HIGHWAY Müller returned to the

"Lehrstück," the form he had taken leave from in a letter of 1977 to Rainer Steinweg, the noted theoretician of the Lehrstück: ". . . I think we have to say 'goodbye' to the Lehrstück until the next earthquake . . . In a landscape where the TEACHINGS are buried so deeply, and which is riddled with mines to boot, one must at times push his head into the sand (mud, rock) to look farther." During a discourse with Gregor Edelmann, published in *Theater der Zeit* #2, 1986, East Berlin, Müller commented on his return to the Lehrstück: ". . . I think something is turning around now, something has to change direction. The situation is rife with changes. This is the moment when one can learn again, when one must learn. And so this play-model Lehrstück becomes timely again."

These new texts, however, move away from the abstractions of MAUSER, or the detached, objectifying narration of HORATIAN. They read like inner monologues, or better: a "stream-of-memory" in which a person recalls, or dreams of, moments of extreme crisis and awesome responsibility, reliving the crucible of such an event. Still, Müller's endnote to Part One indicates that he intended a performance mode which does not emphasize the "personal" aspects of the text, but rather uses it as didactic material in which the narrator's role is split between two or more actors. Thus, models will be constructed for/by the performers to investigate an individual's response/action in confrontations which put conscience and responsibility to an ultimate test; models to learn from a dialectics of history where the personal and the societal are inseparably intertwined.

During a discussion about the text, in Paris, Müller said: "Where I come from, everybody has the same corpses buried in the basement . . . Collective corpses. That's what I write about. In my plays, there is no difference anymore between the actors and the spectators. All of them are responsible."

C.W.

VOLOKOLAMSK HIGHWAY (*La Route des Chars*)
Director: Jean Jourdheuil / J. F. Peyret
Theatre M.C. 93 Bobigny, Paris, 1988

1

RUSSIAN GAMBIT
(after a motif from Alexander Bek)

Posted between Moscow and Berlin
At our backs were woods, in front a river
Eleven hundred eighty miles to Berlin
Sixty-seven miles away from Moscow
In fox holes dug into the frozen mud
We were waiting for our combat orders
And for the first snowfall And for the Germans
At day we heard the front At night we saw it
The Germans had what we were lacking tanks
Airplanes the conqueror's scornful arrogance
My Soldiers there had fear and little else
Fear is the soldier's mother and the first
Cut will bisect the umbilical cord
Who misses it will die of the mother
My Soldiers had just left the schoolyard
In movies they had seen the war
Now I was their commander and my fear was
The fear of their fear And the front was moving
Closer and from the front deserters came
Where are you coming from Comrades
                                    The pocket
The German Did you see him What's he like
The German Did you see him We have seen him
He's a horizon made of tanks the German
That's moving towards you Like this A sky
Of airplanes is the German And a carpet
Of bombs that's covering all of Russia
You'll see him soon enough Before you wake up
From your next sleep Maybe you won't wake up
From your next sleep
                        Why in such a hurry Stay
Recover from the front Tell us Comrades
That's how they talked around the campfires
I heard them and I read in orders from

The regimental staff that Hitler tells
The world it's just a promenade to Moscow
The Red Army has been annihilated
My finger followed carefully each line and
My hands were grasping hard the sheets of paper
The words they burst and flashed inside my head
Like lightning and I knew it without thinking
Their march to Moscow is a promenade
If we are beaten and I also knew
We aren't beaten by their rolling tanks
Not by their airplanes nor their carpet bombing
We're beaten by a general called Fear
And only if we beat him will we conquer
I saw the river It would have been pretty
With leaves maybe and floating flowers I
Thought it's too shallow Not an obstacle
For Germans And the woods across the water
A painter maybe would have loved them I
Hated each tree and every shrub in it
Because it offered cover to the Germans
One should tear up this forest by its roots
And then again the talking at the fires
We're coming from the front We're hungry Comrades
Tell us about the front and eat your fill
What should we tell It will be here tomorrow
The front Then you can hold your wedding with
The German you are itching for
                        Wedding
We'll make it hot enough for him
                        Watch out
That he won't burn and skin your hide
I stood there heard their talking and their laughter
It sounded hollow as from corpses' bellies
And in the gray of dawn I saw their faces
Gray and said What tune is this you're singing
Are you still soldiers or just wailing women
And who told you to take leave from the front
The German they said and their laughter stopped
I said You should be stood against the wall

Yes they said if there is a wall left standing
My hand already reached for the revolver
But then I heard my own voice speaking Eat
From our food and then you will march back
Straight to the front if you think that your life
Is still of value to you or your death
If I see you tomorrow here it will be
The wall and if it is the last left standing
They didn't turn and go back to the front
At night they disappeared direction Moscow
And others came with faces just as gray
And spread their fear I knew I had to pull
The weed or it would sprout a German relish
Love for a life that's free of war or death
A love which makes deserters out of soldiers
I know the day and I shall always know it
It will stay burned into my memory
With those two volleys I shall always hear
Till I'm given my three shovels earth
The front came closer Thinly snow was falling
On my rounds through the trenches the wind blew
Into my nose the putrid stench of fear
That chilled and grabbed my soldiers by their throats
Into my ear their whisper
                              Watch the German
The German won't attack where you expect it
He doesn't like that
                        And what does he like
The German
            Grabs you with a pincers movement
And then
              It's everybody for himself
And pray that you then find a forest handy
Or you'll have no friends left Only the forest
Is your friend The German wouldn't enter
You understand He's got respect for woods
The German
              New songs from the pocket front
Worn down I thought Worn down by the German

The war has barely started They are finished
One should knock them on their heads and yet
One would rather like to stroke their heads
I hadn't ever lost my memory
Of my first battle and of my fear in
My foxhole when I looked at my first tank
Hiding the sky to bury me beneath
And later drag its wheel tracks through my sleep
Until that other first-time-ever moment
A tank before me all ablaze in flames
Struck by the lightning which came from my hand
Scum I thought You're devouring our bread
And feed my soldiers with your fear
You should be taken and shot on the spot
I knew that only terror dispels fear
I saw steel gleaming in the underbrush
At riverside a machine gunner hidden
Alright I asked And he It's quite alright
The bride is dressed up for the wedding but
The bridegroom seems to be delayed the German
I hadn't any other language left
I aimed and emptied the gun belt into
The river like it was a German river
The water danced When will we play this tune
To make the Germans dance When will we see
The river water red from German blood
I shouted now Alarm and Take up arms
A shout went up The Germans like an echo
That mountain sides are throwing at each other
It was less like a shout more like a whisper
That ran along the trenches in one breath

As if they were already next to us
The Germans From the trenches soldiers jumped
Dived back in and jumped out again as if
They were puppets controlled and pulled by wires
Then the first one ran to the woods He wasn't
The last All of them followed him Till one
Called Stop And it was not my voice I stood
Next to myself and stared at the performance

My hand at the machine gun I had used
On my stage between riverside and woods
To play the German part and with tremendous
Success My soldiers rout was the applause
Since I on cue was at a loss for words
Eleven hundred eighty miles to Berlin
Sixty-seven miles away from Moscow
Not till the first of them came to a halt
Held by that voice which firmly shouted Stop
And turned around and stood before me like
Converted pagans between fear and shame
While others kept on running I did notice
My hurting hand burned by the barrel's steel
I sat in my dugout stared at the ground
My face between my hands and I thought hard
How could I turn this mob of men into
A combat unit before their first battle
Then the lieutenant came and time stood still
Comrade Commander one of the squad leaders
He ran into the forest with the others
But that is not the worst
                Not the worst
What else
         He shot himself—in his hand
I see Shot through his hand Anything else
Nothing Comrade Commander
                An accident
Comrade Commander it was no accident
And what did you do Did you shoot the man
I bandaged him And I arrested him
He's waiting outside
           I don't want to see him
And why didn't you shoot him
               I I don't
Don't know
        And I'm supposed to know it, am I
Bring him in then
             Comrade Commander
I do apologize

            Tell me the truth
It was an accident I don't know why
I stumbled when I ran into the woods
I ran into the woods with all the others
That wasn't right One shouldn't run away from
The enemy And yet Comrade Commander
You know yourself it was a practice drill
There was no German anywhere
                              A drill
I see And that shot in your hand it is
The right one isn't it was a drill too
You didn't shirk did you And to the bone
You've practiced haven't you It's hurting
                                    Yes
Comrade Commander
                        You might not be able
To use that hand now any longer and
Maybe the war can't use you any longer
With one hand less than soldiers need in combat
Maybe Comrade Commander
                          Stop it will you
You liar Get out of my sight No stay
Shall I tell you what you are What you are is
A coward and a traitor of your country
The wound's still bleeding That was a neat shot
This is the last time you'll see your blood
The blood you've wasted And it wasn't for us
Within one hour you shall have your peace
For you there won't be any German bullet
Comrade Lieutenant Take the man away
I don't want to see him anymore
His squad shall shoot him before the battalion
Within the hour That's my orders. The
Lieutenant asked me Do we have that right
I said My orders will be executed
If it's not right I can be shot thereafter
You're writing the report Comrade Lieutenant
That hour felt as long as all my life
And his hour was sixty minutes short

Every minute an eternity
An open square was formed by the battalion
And no face was like any other face
But on my orders they presented arms
With one sound like one rifle And I felt
Something like pride in me This mob of men
From town and steppe will be a battalion
And I felt shame in me about my pride
Sadness and anger Do you need a death
Or need to witness how a man is dying
So a battalion will be a battalion
In front of it the man who was to die
Because I gave the order that he'll die
What other order should I have pronounced
Eleven hundred eighty miles to Berlin
Sixty-seven miles away from Moscow
My soldiers trembling since the enemy
Is close who had half Europe under heel
The firing squad fell in The squad he had
Been leader of and hadn't been a leader
Because he couldn't give himself an order
In his one short moment of cowardice
He searched in all their faces with his eyes
That showed us gray the knowledge of his death
A thousand eyes were looking right through him
As if he were translucent before death
He couldn't find a place to rest his hands
The right one stiff wrapped in a bloody bandage
No belt nor rifle nor his badge of rank
No next man in the line to shelter him
And neither did he have a God to share
With Him his death he faced now all alone
Without a country to remember him
I stood in his coat freezing in the wind
The noise the front made sounded like a love song
And then not opening his lips he spoke
And he saluted with his mangled hand
Comrade Commander Would you please forgive me
And send me to the front so I can fight

I said Take off the coat Because it is
A soldier's coat You stopped being a soldier
And with three fingers of his mangled hand
He very slowly unbuttoned his coat
The squad took up their rifles and took aim
And waited that I gave the order Fire
The soldiers' backs and the unsteady aiming
Of their rifles asked the question Why
I felt as if even the wind stood still
Then it became a storm within my head
And then not opening my lips I spoke
Put on your coat again and I He asked
The coat So I shall not be shot
And I Resume your post You'll fight won't you
And Yes Sure I shall fight said he
And tried to put his coat on couldn't find
With his bandaged hand the way into the sleeve
He laughed with us freed of the awful burden
Which had been pressing on him for an hour
With all the weight of earth to cover him
Ten hands were grabbing at his coat and pulling
So his hand would search into the sleeve And back
And forth and there was no end to their laughter
Then broke the film and my command wiped out
The image Fire And the volley cracked
From twelve rifles like one single shot
There was no louder shot during this war
That volley was the pride of their commander
And in his uniform my other I
Wanted to beg the dead man to forgive me
For his death which had been my work
As he had earlier begged me to offer
Another death to him than one in shame
For his moment of cowardice Something
Pulled my hand saluting to my helmet
Belated answer to his last salute
With mangled hand and no helmet to touch
Mercy for traitors is equal to treason
Said the commander hand at his revolver

Give back to him the coat and bury him
That was the first step my battalion took
On our way from Moscow to Berlin
And always does the dead man take my steps
I breathe and eat and drink and sleep at night
But in my head the war does never end
One volley followed by another volley
They echo back and forth between my temples
The medals on my breast glow like white heat
When lips not opening he begins to speak
And lifts his mangled hand saluting me
He whom I ordered shot by martial law
As coward and as traitor to his country
October of the war year forty-one
Eleven hundred eighty miles to Berlin
Sixty-seven miles away from Moscow

Production Note: The part of the Commander should be cast with two performers if at all feasible, with an actor (K1) who has the approximate age of the storyteller, that is, can play his age, and a young actor or actress (K2). K1 is dressed in civilian clothes, K2 in uniform. The actors should be capable of alternating. The distribution of text between K1 and K2 is to be worked out in rehearsal. Separation of image and sound: the weapons have to be seen, the volleys heard, the place of the spectator is between weapon and target. The wishful image of the deserter's pardon needs the same degree of realism as the execution, so that a war can be perceived when a pardon to serve at the front represents the realistic solution. In the shadow of nuclear war, Capitalism's alternative to Communism, it appears as a utopia. Formally, the text is based on the short drama of Pushkin, the Russian variant of *le tragédie classique.*

H.M., 1985

2

FOREST NEAR MOSCOW
(after a motif from Alexander Bek)

A week into the battle for Moscow
And my battalion but a company
Our division routed staff Godknowswhere
The Germans everywhere and nowhere We
Were marching through the woods like blinded chicken
Where's the division fighting Where the Germans
At night the ground froze and hoarfrost at dawn
It fell as rain from trees and helmet rims
At midday when the sun shone on the woods
It drenched the uniforms the soldiers' packs
And turned to mire which clung to the boots
The ambulance was our only burden
That slowly became lighter Every day
Another death And heavier while lighter
With each one who ceased being our burden
No trace of friend or foe nothing but woods
Even the guns were silent for one night
At dawn they found their voice again The new
Uproar of battle brought us certainty
The Germans were at our back and there
Fought the division or what's left of it
On all the highways passing our forest
German reserves were rolling toward Moscow
Our battalion was the only island
Within this German sea of tanks and cannon
Any retreat any advance cut off
A finger looking for its hand which maybe
No arm is joined to any longer
Its body blinded by exploding shells
The soldiers' looks were mutely asking me
Their eyes were holes cut deeply in their faces
And hunger had their cheekbones crosshatched
Commander say where did you lead us to
And mutely I passed on their silent question

Why had we to retreat In our lifetime
The word didn't exist Retreat Why now
And what or who robbed us of our strength
And when did it begin what now is with us
And how And who is guilty In the country
The enemy instead us chasing him
How did you lead us Comrade Stalin
And then my teeth much faster than my tongue
Crunched my answer blood was in my mouth
A soldier stood before me
                        We are hungry
I'm your Commander Don't talk to me like this
Now put your uniform in order and
Come back and tell me what you want to say
He turned and took ten steps as he was ordered
Buttoned his uniform washed off his boots in
A puddle and cleaned with one sleeve his helmet
Then he came back his hand raised in salute
Comrade Commander we are very hungry
There's nothing I can give you for your hunger
Cut me to pieces if you like That's all
Yessir Cut you to pieces Very good
Comrade Commander our ambulance
What's that What's wrong with our ambulance
The ambulance has fallen far behind
Lost Somewhere in the woods way back The doctor
Where is the doctor Sits there at the tree
He's resting Doctor where are our wounded
Won't you get up when I am talking to you
I ask you please don't scream at me I am
An officer like you Battalion's Surgeon
Yes I am asking the battalion's surgeon
Where is the ambulance Battalion's Surgeon
I am a Captain Comrade First Lieutenant
I'm asking once again don't scream at me
I didn't ask about your rank or badge
I asked about the ambulance Where is it
Am I the driver How should I know where
The ambulance It has fallen behind

And we kept marching on They'll soon catch up
Our battalion's surgeon Comrades has
Abandoned our wounded men and left
The ambulance he was entrusted with
A coward he betrayed dishonorably
Those who have shed their blood for our country
Betrayed Are you saying to me Betrayed
And who has led us then into this trap
Who's chasing us in all directions through
These woods Maybe in circles all the time
You see yourself the men are close to collapse
Your leadership has pushed them to the brink
Their mess tins empty not one ounce of bread left
Soon we shall crawl on our hands and knees
Like beetles waiting for the fatal boot step
Comrade Commander I would like to ask you
Could you divulge to the battalion or
What's left of it thanks to your leadership
Where you will lead us now What's your intention
Before the enemy shall wipe us out
And fifty soldiers stood behind me and
Their looks were piercing holes into my back
Like fifty daggers from a hundred eyes
I couldn't bear it any more and turned
To my battalion shrunk to a company
After a week of combat led by me
Led And where What kind of leader am I
In narrow eye slits I could see that question
Eyes from the steppe transparent and of
Its grass eyes gray from steel-dust green from wind
Eyes shortsighted behind their thickish lenses
We're reeling through the woods like drunken gypsies
Are you still the commander Are we soldiers
And who will save us from this devastation
There was something in me that tried to scream
What do you want Who am I What do I know
I: Something slowly walked toward the soldiers
To disappear in that mass in those bodies
That these eyes won't look at me anymore

I saw with horror how they backed away
Chary of me as if I were a threat
I turned around a puppet pulled by strings
Looked at the doctor A hundred eyes were seeing
With my eyes how his hands were fluttering
And without voice or was it now the voice
Of the battalion like a roar or whisper
That I heard from afar I said to him
Before the enemy wipes us out
We're going to wipe out the enemy And
Do you believe what you just said Commander
My fear was asking deep down in myself
And now we'll march back all the way and search
With empty mess tins and no ounce of bread left
And even if we crawl on hands and knees
The ambulance that the battalion's surgeon
Abandoned the dishonorable coward
Because we shall leave to the enemy
No man nor car nor weapon nor a corpse
As long as we have one breath left But first
We shall take care of our problem here
Captain Belenkhov you have been demoted
The reason Negligence of duty as
A doctor and an officer because
Of cowardice Take off your epaulets
You know you cannot do this You're a First
Lieutenant I'm a Captain You don't have
The right Only the People's Commissar
I am a medical school graduate
He was correct I looked down at my hands
They itched to grab him close around his neck
They itched to have at least in one fast move
Ripped off his epaulets from both his shoulders
The only part of him that was still clean
He used to polish them at every stop
Being a medical school graduate
My hands however were tied fast as if
With chains nay faster even than with chains
To Soviet law To our martial law

The commissar the court of the division
They could demote the coward maybe even
Put him before a firing squad Were I
The commissar the court of the division
What will become of our Soviet order
If I take the law into my own hands
The rights of millions Soviet citizens
How much are left of us The Soviet order
What's left of it in front of German tanks
Take it in my two hands that have the power
Power over a company that yester-
Day was still a battalion and tomorrow
Maybe is nothing but a victory
Report in some issue of German newsreels
In my two hands which alien and naked
Protrude from my Commander's uniform
And can I be sure that my soldiers there
Aren't just waiting until their commander
Makes some mistake now or maybe later
Another day like this trapped in the forest
And they will know no enemy but death
They're standing there like trees before the storm
Or I'm the tree that stands before the storm
And look at me their eyes like stones Well now
How will you get yourself out of this fix
Comrade Commander Martial law that's it
The Soviet order Do you see now that
You the commander are a little cog
A tiny screw in our Soviet order
And scars are looking at me of wounds old
And new Wounds that were made with paper or
With typewriters and cadre files in our
State offices and councils on behalf
Of Soviet order our Soviet order
Not counting scars made by interrogations
Who tells me that these soldiers wouldn't move
Covered with scars that scream aloud for wounds
Many have in their heart a grave without
A name Who tells me that one of them wouldn't

Take the law in both his hands and then
Making short shrift break it across his knee
With hunger crazed maybe or since the Germans
Begin to squeeze and clean the trap we're in
And rip the epaulets off both my shoulders
Of the commander who has poorly led
YOU LED US TO OUR DEATH NOW LEAD NO MORE
And everyone will be his own commander
In my poor image if today I'm not
Able to give an order to my hands
But take the law under my boot because
My blood is boiling when I think of it
That somewhere in these endless no man's woods
Passed by the enemy reaching for Moscow
On this one island in the German sea
That on four sides conflagrates our country
Stands our ambulance lost and forgotten
Bleed our comrades And right here before me
In his eyes fear but not for our comrades
His fluttering hands shielding his epaulets
As if some private parts need to be covered
Dances a ballet the battalion's surgeon
A captain he of our Soviet army
Afraid to lose the ground beneath his feet
To lose the rank protecting him from death
Longer maybe than that man under him
On his abyss the Private Belenkhov
Why don't you choke I thought of your degree
From medical school Captain Sir And Who
Did pay for your tuition Comrade Captain
And martial law is manacling my hands
And it is I who's choking on his duty
And deep in me a doubt began to speak
It's the battalion's surgeon who deserted
The ambulance entrusted to his care
But who did lead then the battalion
Into these woods which won't have any exit
But to the German army's tanks and cannon
Maybe you also should rip off your two

Epaulets from your shoulders right away
Comrade Commander who was a bad leader
What are they to you our wounded men
A knife stuck in your breast or in your back
A pain Comrade or are they but a fear
I thought about it chewing on my tongue
The distant noise of tanks was in my ears
The roar of bombs and of artillery
As long as we are dying we are fighting
As long as we are fighting Germans die
Who has more blood to shed we or they
I slowly counted with my eyes the soldiers
How many of them will die Who and who
When we break out of this trap And maybe
We'll never make it ever out of it
And our bones forever will grow roots here
In this no man's wood on this little island
Passed by the enemy reaching for Moscow
My thoughts went helter-skelter in my head
The Soviet order what of it I thought
When the Soviet Union disappears
Stop playing devil's advocate Comrade
The very ground beneath your boots that is
The Soviet Union Soviet order lives
Within your heart and also in your brain
And if it's only empty tanks which crash
Into each other on this wasted earth
And if we go on fighting in the clouds
Where memories of our dead are living
And Captain I said Captain Belenkhov
Of this battalion I am the commander
As long as we are cut off from the army
In this forest that is a single island
With the German sea burning the country
A Soviet island and a Soviet forest
Maybe we won't live to see other forests
Nor the division nor the fatherland
And the battalion is the Soviet army
This ground here under our boots is called

The Soviet Union and I'm Soviet law
You will do service as Private Belenkhov
And you will carry from enemy fire
On your shoulders without epaulets
The battlefield your university
Till our guns are silent in Berlin
Our wounded men Soldier Belenkhov
And now take off your epaulets
Before I rip them off your shoulders

1985

3

THE DUEL
(after a motif from Anna Seghers)

It was in June in that black month in the
Fifth year of the Republic Which we soon
Erased in our calendar It was
A month of joy for our enemies
Since it was nearly our very last year
And could have even been the first year of
The final war if we had not been born
Again by Soviet tanks a second time
I sat behind my desk in my office
At V. E. B. OCTOBER or was it PROGRESS
Outside vox populi RUSSKI GO HOME
FREEDOM and OFF WITH THE GOATEE and also
GERMANY ABOVE ALL NATIONS
In front of me balancing on his chair's edge
My deputy and on my desk between us
The sign that had been at my office door
Spelling my name beneath the word DIRECTOR
It was removed by my own deputy
Quite like a declaration of war And
I saw him balancing six years ago on
Another chair's edge and between us was
No desk that time and no sign with my name
Only a world war and ten years in prison
The rain kept drumming on the barracks' roof
His jacket was a former army tunic
My suit of worsted cloth from Nazi stock.
Why won't you let me be the way I am
Not in my life will I be engineer
Even if you drag me through forty schools.
I am a worker Let me stay the way
I am Is this what you did say when you
Put on that tunic when it was field gray
You've dyed it black meanwhile Are you in mourning
You'll go to school and if I need to drag you

By both your ears into the lecture hall.
And now he sat before me My deputy
As delegate of the STRIKE COMMITTEE
Licking the blood that's dripping from his finger
His declaration of war right between us
The sign with my name from my office door.
You have forgotten how to use your hands
I thought you've men to do such work for you
A leader must know how to delegate
You want to join the working class again
Why don't you now But behind iron bars
What committee is this What sort of strike
Is this a joke Or do you want my chair
You've been my deputy quite long enough
To know how you could stab me in the back
Through proper channels while your hands stay clean
So you won't need that screaming mob out there
Egged on by the West.
                    You take it easy
Egged on by the West That screaming mob
Out there Why don't you call them lumpen Rabble.
Who's striking against whom Where are we living.
There is the window if you'd like to see it.
I see him on his schoolbench sweating blood
And water in his fight with mathematics
They wouldn't go into his stubborn skull.
I won't make it I'll never understand it
And what I do know I won't when in class
And of exams I rather wouldn't talk
Our professor said It is genetic
One person's got it and the other doesn't
And cobblers shouldn't leave their boot tree Said he
And we'll need workers too Why did you never
Want to believe me when I told you so
That I won't ever be an engineer.
So that's what you would like Said I And your
What is the name of that professor of yours
I'll show him where the hammer hits these days.
And right away I recognized his voice

Unchanged by thirteen years of history
At Dresden college Nineteenthirtyfour
Stormtroopers marching outside We were sweating
Over equations Then the signature
They pushed a paper in front of our nose
JEWS AND COMMUNISTS WILL BE EXPELLED
Who signs will stay You've picked mathematics
My university was prison and
The two-times-two of sheer survival was
My mathematics twenty terms and more.
WORKERS AND FARMERS COLLEGE What a joke
That's like vivisection if you ask me
I won't claim that intellect is merely
Genetic Yet you think the way you grow up
This will take generations Nature won't
Jump hurdles.
    Well, we aren't nature, are we?
Let's wait and see it The professor said
He hadn't recognized my voice.
My deputy opened the window wide
You smell the smoke NEW GERMANY is burning.
He laughed while I grabbed for the telephone.
Your final argument Call the police
You only can denounce me to yourself
All your comrades have gone underground
Just hear the static in the deadened wire.
I saw him in his class when he was mocked
Because equations turned his brain to mush
I sat with him the night before his finals
It was a duel My enemy his teacher
Whose advantage was his signature
Twenty terms or more of mathematics
My weapon he who's head wouldn't accept it
I thought who's face is this clown's ugly mug
That's spouting forth those long interred words
STRIKE COMMITTEE GENERAL STRIKE and who's
Are those heavy jowls the bulging tummy
The trace of bonuses and compromise
I saw a long forgotten image rising

A bricklayer made minister of state
From Spain to prison camps then to high office
On his desk top he stood and sang and didn't
Stop singing until they took him away
From government house to the hospital
Straight from his desk into the loony bin
He sang among the files accounts and papers
His song of Spain MADRID THE BEAUTIFUL
And as the medics tied him to the stretcher
'Twas half a scream and half a whisper Give me
A gun and point the enemy out to me
A victim of the paper wars you'd say
Who's fallen at the bureaucratic front
As for myself I never had seen Spain
Neither the red side nor the black one Gray
Are all the colors behind prison walls
So I took off my tie and then my jacket
NEW GERMANY's smoke in my nostrils and
In my ears my deputy's loud laughter
He who was my creation and that Spanish
Song of the comrade in the loony bin
I'll show you where God lives.
                        Stalin is dead.
You know what you're saying.
                        Don't you know.
I put the tie on slipped into my jacket
Something was choking me A lump of time
And now Where are the tanks I thought
They must arrive and they will be arriving
They which gave birth to us in Forty-five
A second time now with their smell of oil
Of heated steel and soldiers' sweat When smoke
Is in the air I knew from memory
The tanks will come Why aren't they here now
They have to come and they will without fail
The tanks the last of our arguments
And as I thought this I was also thinking
Four years in power and that's what we've come to
The last of our arguments the tanks

And out there all the world passes us by
From Cuba to Cambodia and so forth
We stared in silence at each others mask
And each of us alone now in his skin
And suddenly we heard the quiet outside
Then they came He was the first to hear them
I could clearly see it in his eyes.
And so we're taken to the breast again
The wet nurse she is on her way She's riding
T Thirtyfours and she has milk for all
And some will like it and some others won't
But suckled they will be And I I should
Have known Should have known better right away
One time is no time What The Russian tanks
Midwives of the German Workers State
Did I say Stalin's dead Heil Comrade Stalin
There he is The specter in the turret
Beneath the tank tracks Red Rosa is rotting
As large as Berlin We're the gravediggers
Each one where he belongs to do his piece work
We know the way you're feasting with your specters
The night is shorter at the buffet supper.
Here is paper Now sit on your behind
And write your self critique You know the text.
First show your face and then apply cosmetics
I know the bible Said he and already
Sat at my desk Who signs will stay
Was that it As I saw his back and shoulders
Stooped over my desk and the sheet of paper
And as the pause before his signature
Took twenty years according to my watch
I longed to be back in my prison cell
At Brandenburg prison the first time ever
For one beat of my heart He handed me
The paper with his signature I threw
The sign into the wastepaper basket
His declaration of war And I fished
It out again from the wastepaper basket
And stuffed it in my jacket and I stuffed

His self critique into the selfsame pocket
Through the open window blew the smell
Of sour ashes of extinguished fires
Of trees and metal and of dogshit
And in the gray sky of Berlin there danced
Black flakes of paper torn and burned
We didn't look into each other's eyes
We wiped each one of us his hand at his
Lapel after the parting handshake Then
We both went back to our work

1986

4

CENTAURS*
(a Horror Tale from the Saxonian of Gregor Samsa)

MIRANDA:

O brave new world,
That has such people in it!
PROSPERO:

'Tis new to thee.

I had a dream last night It was a nightmare
Then I woke up and all things were in order.
Comrade Super everything's in order
No incident no disorderly conduct
And not a single crime The people are
As they appear in books and in the papers.
I'd like to see that No I'd rather not
This is the end You know what you are saying
Have you gone crazy No reason to panic
It is an error It's a conspiracy
And you're its tool You know it or you don't
To live or not to live that is the question.
I don't know what you mean It is the truth
We've done it after all Comrade Super
Ten years of day and night shifts not for nothing
Security and order that was it
What we were taught and that was our goal.
Yes and awareness And where others have
Awareness you have nothing but a hole
Maybe you're only an objective enemy
There is probation for stupidity
For in-house-use I'll tell you We produce
Security and order

And awareness.
Yes and awareness Right And the mother
Of order is disorderly conduct
The father of State Security is

---

*Centaur: Old Greek for Red Tape. (H.M.)

None other than the same State's Enemy
And should the light once shine in every brain
We're left behind sitting on our awareness
The game is Cops and Robbers It has rules
Rule number one is One hand washes the
Other hand I'd like to see the person
Who washes both his hands with one hand only
In short Cops and robbers are a dia
Lectical unit Our daily bread
Is misdemeanor Murder Sunday dinner
And our state's a grinder that must grind
The state needs enemies like grinders grain
A state without an enemy is not
A state A kingdom for an enemy
Who would need us when all things are in order
I'd go and hack my desk to firewood
And use the staff-files here to kindle it
We'd have to take off our uniform
And put it on a hook And ourselves
We'd hang on top of it If the hook holds
What are you doing.
                 Take off my uniform.
You are on duty not on Nudist Beach
What are you looking for.
                   Rope and hook.
When you're off-duty you can hang yourself
First you will make amends for your mistake
You did retreat when you were facing facts
And soon lost sight of our sacred truth
By your blind faith in what your eyes were seeing
A fact is not a fact if we won't say so
Why else then do we wear a uniform
And wear a brain under the cap Being
Determines consciousness in class history
In Socialism it's the opposite
What's needed here is quite another fire
Than one you could start with a chopped up desk
Or from a laundry basket filled with files
And when you have corrected your mistake

You needn't hang yourself when you're off-duty
A medal's what you get And a bonus
Now go and drive across the intersection
When all the lights are red.
                  At red across
The intersection I.
             And you'll be
In uniform And that is an order.
In uniform when all is red across.
If you don't care to get a medal and
No bonus either Are you an animal
What have we done What shall become of us
If our strongest weapon doesn't work
The economic leverage Now think
Of your official oath End of discussion.
What my official oath says is At red
Across an intersection is a mis
Demeanor And my consciousness tells me
It's risking human lives.
It is a matter
Of principle Who cares for human lives
All of us have to sacrifice And let's
Assume the human life is yours When you're
On duty it is our life that's snuffed
Out on that intersection And a statue
Will be yours plus medal and the bonus
And if you're worried by your oath of office
No one forbids you to report yourself
My oath of office tells me I'll report you
If at red you cross the intersection
But the rabbit doesn't chase the dog
First the offense and later the report
And our crisis now demands that someone
At red will drive across that intersection
He drove at red across the intersection
In uniform On duty In rush hour
There went the Ninth Symphony of police cars
With whistles and with sirens it was shrieking
Into each ear Ablaze the intersection

I could see the reflection from my desk
Like a beacon I bit into the desk
So that I wouldn't loudly shout in triumph
About such criminal offense on duty
And clasped my legs with both my arms so they
Wouldn't start a stomping dance of joy
In uniform I doffed my cap in mourning
Comrade you didn't die without a cause
You've fallen at the front of dialectics
How do you solve a contradiction By
Stepping right into it and straight ahead
Not looking right or left and it will split you
Like Jesus whom the cross has torn apart
Or Prometheus whom his rock exploded
We'll have to hush up and dress up his death
A statue for The Unknown Keeper of
The Law Not everything that serves the masses
Is understood by the same masses Not
At once at least And suddenly there stood
Right on my desk top our honored corpse
Brand new the uniform the epaulets
Already sprouted into angels' wings.
Comrade Super everything's in order
The dialectics has been re-established
And all systems now are back to normal.
He stooped down and sang into my ear
Stalin shall fetch me if I ever know
What he tried to tell me Something like
Alas The hobbyhorse's back is broken
Got up and turned on toes a pirouette
Flew out the window flapping twice his wings
And when I tried to get up tried to see
How he took flight something like lightning struck
Me down with pain like from a welding torch
I and my desk had grown to form one body
Into one body grew my desk and I
I pulled and tore A struggle with all fours
The desk around my belly no lifesaver
That's how consciousness gets us all stuck

My desk is Caucasus and Cross of mine
The dream of the Commune: Not I but We
So that's it Is that really all there is
The function's wedding with the functionary
Until death do us part And maybe
Dying won't happen to us any more
But mankind's dream of an eternal life
Now immortality you will be mine
Was this my desk or was this I myself
Who told you so Old Prussian my friend
If it is fireproofed and well cared for
And all repairs done by authorized service
The Socialist desk will be our backpack
Into the Communist Millenium
We'll have to train for the new canter Left
And left And every step competitive
I Am a Man a Man Who's Like an Oaktree
What's the next line Was it Maybe I will be
I think I have forgotten how to sing
A frog is in my throat A Corpse Tomorr . . .
I and my desk Who is who's property
The desk is people's property And what
Am I Below a desk above a human
No human being but a humachine
A furnitureman or a manfurniture
The staff files are my abdominal organs
I'm an occurrence To be put on file
Oh combined billet of oakwood and flesh
How does a desk shit And what does it eat
Does it perform its matrimonial duties
And if a desk would like to fuck a desk
What will come of it A desk and a desk
A desk and a desk and a desk and a desk
Beautiful lady may I ask But how
Do you recognize the other gender
We need law and order after all
A carousel is turning in my head
My ID card Do I have to change it
Are we Comrades or one Comrade only

And why is my mouth watering when I
See the list of ordinances at
The wall and on your wooden top Did I
Say on your wooden top now It is ours
The telephonebook Hunger my old desk
And what off-duty means we can forget it
Work and leisure won't compete no more
That's Chapter Three of human history
On hands and knees towards the upright posture
The quantum leap towards the class position
Each one his own monument so to speak
Class consciousness will be the pedestal
Knock wood And dialects at attention
Sacred the solving of all contradictions
Ah Ink It truly is a special juice
No alcohol on duty And No smoking
Special occurrences There were none Law
And cleanliness Security And clean . .
Service For dinner I will have a file
And then a desk for Well For reproduction
. . . Liness Security And clean . . . What's ticking
In our wood Hey It's the death tick Help

5

THE FOUNDLING

(after Kleist)

He sat and faced me during visiting hours
All my five years at Bautzen penitentiary
He talked to me IN MARXANDENGELSTONGUES
About his workers paradise I watched
The way his lips moved and between the teeth
His tongue the sweat on his forehead and when
He really got going tears And what
He said was as it wasn't ever said
Since I had moved to Bautzen from Berlin
During a summernight never forgotten
In Nineteensixtyeight Year of the Tanks
And in five years I didn't say one word
And not one syllable during his visits
But I did him a favor and accepted
The presents he had brought me And his back
Was more bent each time when he walked away
Back to his hell that was his paradise
I was allowed back to my prison cell
And there I learned what's needed to survive
Eating glass or chewing razor blades
For instance will suspend the prison rules
My second move happened with proper papers
With Do you really know what you are doing
Here you have housing work security
There Man won't count but only capital
And this with my wounds which are breaking open
Again each time they point with fingers at
My scars And now I am in West Berlin
Half-city of the old and the new widows
Corpses in closets money in the bank
Corpses with David's star In brown In armygray
Mangled by metal Cooked to mush in tanks
Smoke through the chimney Dust from carpet bombings
Plötzensee monument on butcher hooks

The plaque that disappeared at Landwehr canal
The latest grave harbors the pipe dream of
A Socialism without guns and tanks
They take care of their graves their dogs their cats
And of their bank account The corpse is lively
To paradise go those who can afford it
And I I'm death I come from Asia
The knife sticks in there but the heart keeps beating
Homesick spells nausea spells hemorrage
It rained when I was standing at his door
Hand on the doorbell dripping A wet dog
I saw his shadow with the light behind him
Do you know what's the time There are still people
Who need their sleep so they can go to work
And your mother You know she is ill
But you don't care I know that well enough
And what is wearing down her life is you
Not you They're looking for me It's that handbill
He didn't ask Who and What kind of handbill
And if you'd like to know what kind of handbill
You're drunk Go home to bed And sleep the booze off
Against the brother-armies' intervention
That's what they call it I've a brother too
In Prague That is I had a brother once
In Prague He is a pile of ashes now
A bunch of bones and smell of flesh that's burned
He burned himself to death in Prague my brother
Madmen are everywhere
                                        Madmen
I know who's mad around here
                                        Do you know that
Then you know what's going to happen now
I'm not just anyone You aren't either
And even if I'd like to I cannot
Pretend to myself and not to the party
That I didn't hear what you confessed
Confessed he said And I Confessed If someone
Is going to confess here it is you
Comrade Father Who is not my father

How often have I wished you'd be my father
And not the Comrade who adopted me
My enemy in every proxy war
You people waged for your sacred cause
The wars against long hair and jeans and jazz
With Putyourhandsup at the police precinct
Facing the wall and standing till you fainted
What your cause is I know it better now
With tracks of tanks you've written on the bodies
Of OUR PEOPLE what you called your cause
Why don't you take your coat off You are soaked
Put my jacket on It fits you Does it
I don't think that your jacket's fitting me
I picked you from the ruins once A bundle
Of misery I came back from the camps
My genitals smashed to a pulp No child
For me You were my future Did we ever
Deny you anything And that's your thanks
The swastika in Leipzig at the blackboard
In Dresden at the bridge your scrawled graffiti
FREEDOM and RUSSKIES OUT Freedom for whom
That rated ten years in prison among friends
For you it meant another school or changing
Your university You ought to thank
Your mother on your knees The way I was
Crawling on my knees when I begged the party
For your freedom And make haste Her cancer
Won't wait Russkies out What do you know
They would have strung up all of us if we
Hadn't had the tanks and guns behind us
And what then did you lack in all those years
Since I have pulled you from the smoking rubble
I wouldn't like to know who was your father
Perhaps the Nazi who did kick and truncheon
My genitals at roll call in the camp
No children for me Only you Who are you
I know now what you've lacked The truncheon
And you have learned your lesson in the camps
TO EACH HIS OWN and LABOR MAKES YOU FREE

Speak low Behind that door my wife is dying
So you have noticed Has she ever lived
And if you want to know what I have lacked
Since you have PULLED ME FROM THE SMOKING RUBBLE
I wish you would have left me in the ruins
Go ask your wife And if you aren't able
To lift your ass out of the armchair I will
Tell you what she lacked and what I've lacked
Her cancer you should rather call it Comrade
My swastika was also of your schooling
How do you talk with editorials
And how do you embrace a party platform
You tried to pacify me with your presents
Never an answer when I asked you who
Is right and why The jokes people were telling
Or the NEW GERMANY your picture bible
The record player was for Budapest
Yet for my friend shot at the Berlin wall
Nothing would do but a motorcycle
The blue shirt on the seat was like a bonus
For the one I'd torn during flag parade
That morning when I knew my friend was dead
From the red neckcloth to the blue shirt torn
That was my education in your school
The red neckcloth my umbilical cord
Soaked with my tears fifteen years ago
When Stalin died Today I merely laugh
Then tears welled up into my eyes and I
Entered the room where the woman was dying
Who was my mother and who was it not
I listened how she whispered to her cancer
And took my clothes off heavy from the rain
I licked the cold sweat off her waxen forehead
Mixed with my snot and with my tears
I laid my face on her shrivelled breasts
Where now the cancer made itself at home
Her grave already paid for at the graveyard
And then I laid my head in her lap that
Never had been home to me because

I wasn't given birth by any mother
My father just an empty uniform
And sometimes he is on my back a specter
Don't turn around Your father is a butcher
I said I want to be a daughter
FORGOTTEN AND FORGOTTEN AND FORGOTTEN
The Thaelmann Song The Partisans of the
Amur and Onward to the Final Fight
The neckcloth wet from Stalin's memorial service
And the torn blue shirt for the friend who fell
At the Berlin wall Stalin's monument
For Rosa Luxemburg The ghost cities
FORGOTTEN Kronstadt Budapest and Prague
Haunted at night by Communism's specter
Knocking its signals through the cities' plumbing
FORGOTTEN AND FORGOTTEN AND FORGOTTEN
It's always buried by the shit again
And rises once again out of the shit
FORGOTTEN AND FORGOTTEN AND FORGOTTEN
Making its rounds and taking its own course
I didn't cry I hadn't any tears left
I didn't enter where the woman died
I stood in my wet mud-tracks on the carpet
What do I care for your Socialism
It soon will all be drowned in Coca Cola
FORGOTTEN AND FORGOTTEN AND FORGOTTEN
Or for the rib cage of a strange old woman
Why do you let go of the telephone
Don't you recall the number I know it
I haven't yet forgotten it and not
The night I stood there at the phone as you now
That's seven years ago Don't you remember
You came home from a meeting Where they had
Broken your spine And it was very quiet
There in your study You had locked the door
I knew with whom you were alone Did you
See them The columns of your precious dead
All those you've stricken from the calendar
And carefully effaced on photographs

FORGOTTEN AND FORGOTTEN AND FORGOTTEN
How then did you review the grand parade
As last salute the hand at your revolver
Onward Comrades to the final fight
Was your gun's muzzle cold against your temple
Did your hand tremble when it felt the trigger
As my hand did feeling the telephone
And yours does now afraid of the same number
What are you waiting for Comrade Father
No trust in our state's executive
Doubts about Socialist legality
A blot that will disgrace your party file
Why Comrade do you call us only now
If I had waited then as long as you do
Your hero's grave had long been occupied
Why do you take your jacket off I'm cold
You'd like to get out of your uniform
Out from your stranglehold of tie and collar
Do you know you're still human underneath
A self-critique right after each advance
And a new leader's icon at each turn
Perhaps if you would also strip your skin
We've built with our own bones And now you
With your bones and with other people's bones
I know what you have built A prison
Tomorrow when the door is locked behind you
You'll know the difference A prison We
If I had known what you have never told me
The night you came home seven years ago
Back from your meeting with your backbone broken
My best friend shot killed at the Berlin wall
It is behind him I'm still facing it
I hadn't moved a hand for you and not
One single finger And your moment of
Truth THE MIRROR REVEALS THE ENEMY
Had been your last moment The masquerade
Of the dead avantgarde your final film
FORGOTTEN AND FORGOTTEN AND FORGOTTEN
The coup de grace your final party work

He looked at me hand on the telephone
Did I ask you that night to make the phone call
At least I hadn't lived to see this day
You live to see it Don't forget the date
Your revolver is no monopoly
There is no privilege in Socialism
I'm volunteering to be put on file
And my revolver is the mausoleum
Of German Socialism I'm playing
Home free The Wall is people's property
The ammunition which will tear my body
Is people's property and I'm the people
FORGOTTEN AND FORGOTTEN AND FORGOTTEN
What nice coincidence You will be twice
Bereaved No questions when you're wearing black
FORGOTTEN AND FORGOTTEN AND FORGOTTEN
I wish I were my father who's a specter
In uniform who truncheons kicks and kills
FORGOTTEN AND FORGOTTEN AND FORGOTTEN
The last thing I remember was his sobbing
And his voice that tried to scream against it
They shall shoot you You damned Nazibastard
They shall shoot you like a rabid dog
And the clicking of the phone as he
Picked it up and dialed the number

VOLOKOLAMSK HIGHWAY is, after GERMANIA and CE-MENT, the third effort at Proletarian tragedy in the age of counter-revolution that will end with the fusion of Man and Machine, the next step of evolution (which presupposes the revolution and doesn't need drama anymore). The image: Wounded Man who in slow-motion rips off his bandages, who in quick-motion is swathed again with bandages, etc., in perpetuum. Timespace: THE MOMENT OF TRUTH WHEN THE MIRROR / REVEALS THE ENEMY . . . The alternative is the black mirror that doesn't give back anything anymore. The satyr play CENTAURS presents the tragedy as farce.

H. M.

A Letter to Robert Wilson

A LETTER TO ROBERT WILSON was written in February 1987 and published as a supplement to the program brochure for *Death Destruction & Detroit II*, directed and designed by Robert Wilson, which opened February 27, 1987, at the Schaubühne, West Berlin.

According to Wilson, he asked Heiner Müller to write a text for the production, to be based originally on works by Kafka but later on the Tshingis Aitmatov text mentioned in the letter. When Müller encountered difficulties with this project, he wrote Wilson the LETTER instead. Wilson used it in the production along with other texts, among them one by the Austrian poet Konrad Bayer who is referred to by Müller in THE WOUND WOYZECK.

C. W.

For one week I have been trying to produce a text which could serve as a gravitational center to your production of DD&D II, a creation that more than any of your earlier works consists of its own explosion. My effort has failed. Maybe, the explosion already had progressed too far, the degree of its acceleration (I'm not talking of Greenwich time) was already too high, that a text which willy-nilly means something could still inscribe itself in the vortex of the detonation. To speak of progress in connection with an explosion seems paradoxical, but maybe for a long while now the liberation of the dead hasn't been happening in slow-motion anymore but in quick-motion. What remains to be done is the effort of describing my failure so that it will at least become an experience. The starting point was a text by Tshingis Aitmatov that describes a Mongolian torture which served to turn captives into slaves, tools without a memory. The technology was simple: the captive, who had been sentenced to survival and not designated for the slave trade but for domestic use by the conquerors, had his head shaved and covered with a helmet made from the skin of a freshly slaughtered camel's neck. Arms and legs shackled, the neck in the stocks so that he couldn't move the head, exposed on the steppe to the sun which dried the helmet and contracted it around his skull so that the regrowing hair was forced to grow backward into the scalp, the tortured prisoner lost his memory within five days—if he survived them—and was, after this operation, a laborer who didn't cause trouble, a Mankurt. There is no revolution without a memory. An early design of total utilization of labor, until its transformation into raw material in the concentration camps. I couldn't represent this event—the disintegration of thinking, the extinction of memory—only describe it, and any description is silenced, as our experiment with Kafka texts already was, when confronted with the centrifugal force of your images: Literature is experience congealed. The dead are writing with us on the paper of the Future at which flames are already licking from all sides. (Technology merely trains reflexes, it prevents experience. Our camel's skin the computer, it is nothing but the present.) Yesterday I dreamed the end of libraries: next to workmens' barracks and engine rooms where geometrical modules were manufactured—I couldn't figure out their function or possible use— stacks, heaps of books, books in the grass, books in the mud, in the excavated building sites, putrid paper, decomposed letters. On his way to the toilet a worker with an empty face. Another dream of the same night: we were eating, tightly packed at narrow tables, in the spacious inner court of a castle in Switzerland, beneath helicopter flights. Sirens interrupted the meal: air raid warning. A waiter or the castellan in his armor informed us what had triggered it. Seventeen coaches of the Federal Soccer League had run over two children while driving in France. When I tried to translate the news for you, hoping for your coyote-like laughter, I discovered you weren't sitting at the table anymore but standing on the castle's ramparts, harnessed in a spacious steel construction, nearly grown together with it, because of your headphones not reachable by my voice, unreachable also for the sirens of the Swiss air raid warning. Next to my typewriter on the desk which is full of burn marks and hasn't been cleaned up in years, there lies a reproduction, a picture postcard, of Tintoretto's MIRACLE OF MARCUS. Perhaps you have seen the painting in Milan, at the Pinacoteca Brera. I haven't seen it there, maybe it was just being restored, or I cannot remember it and have to be content with the postcard. That offers the advantage of the imprecise view, like at times a bad seat during a performance of yours. (The ideal audience of DD&D II would be one single spectator, enormously stretched between the four playgrounds of the dead in the vault of the stage space, crucified by geometry as in Leonardo's drawing after Vitruvius's text about "homo circularis" and "homo quadratus": "If a man lies on his back, his arms and legs stretched out, and you place your drawing compass's needle at the point of his navel and draw a circle, such a circle will touch the fingertips of both hands and the tips of the toes. As there is a circle to be found at the body, there also will be the figure of the square. Namely, if you take measure from the soles of the feet to the crown of the head and then apply such measure to the stretched out hands, it will result in equal width and height as with surfaces that are laid out in a square by means of a T-square." This One-Person-Audience should have one eye that is attached to a pillar rising from the navel, circular and catholic, or turning with great speed as the eye of a certain reptile whose name I have forgotten. Maybe, it only exists in my dreams.) Back to the Tintoretto: What I'm seeing is a church nave, vaulted by Roman arches, diagonally tapered toward the back, the right wall with its moldings and balconies is fully visible. Two men standing on ladders, the one with his right, the other one with his left hand holding on to the parapet, lower from the foremost balcony a naked old man, maybe a corpse, head first towards the ground. A white cloth with which he probably was clothed serves as a rope: his sex isn't important anymore. A third helper reaches from below for his right arm that is hanging down. He is the only one in the room who is wearing a turban. Behind him a man with arms spread out, expectation or salutation, how does one salute a dead man whose resurrection still is in the future. The left foreground is dominated by the Saint himself. With stretched out left arm he directs—like a foreman the crane—the labor at the balcony that is a deposition from the cross. The right hand holds the tablet or the book with Future's diagram. Before the Saint's feet a gray-white corpse. The skin color of the muscular body is meant to indicate that the soul has already left it: It belongs to art and putrefaction. On the right behind the corpse, a mourning father figure. The dead's head is twisted, as if to avoid the father's blessing hand. Andsoforth the personnel of the legend. The picture's secret is the trap door in the background, held open by two men. From the depths light emanates: the heavens are below. Hit by the light from the depths, the group of figures in the right foreground reels: Two men on their knees, the upper trunks thrown backwards, the faces turned away from each other. The stronger one of the two, head and breast in a different light which emanates from the Saint and the dead man, tries with both his arms to prevent the fall of the second man who, falling, clutches the knees of a woman. The woman is the counterpart of the Saint, one hand in front of her eyes, protection against the imperious gesture of Future's architect or against the light from the underground. The light is a hurricane. Written as the crow flies between the two German capitals Berlin, separated by the chasm of their shared and not shared history, piled up by the latest earthquake as a borderline between two continents. Accept this letter as an expression of my desire to be present in your work.

Heiner Müller
23 February, 1987

''THE END OF THE WORLD
HAS BECOME A FADDISH PROBLEM''

THE END OF THE WORLD . . . is an interview with Uwe Wittstock, printed as ''Why does one make so much money off the End of the World, Herr Müller?,'' in the Sunday Magazine of *Frankfurter Allgemeine Zeitung*, Frankfurt, January 17, 1986. It was published with its present title in the volume *Gesammelte Irrtumer* (Collected Errors), *Interviews and Conversations with Heiner Müller*, Frankfurt, 1986.

Uwe Wittstock is an editor and literary critic of *Frankfurter Allgemeine Zeitung*, West Germany's leading national paper. He also edited volume #73: *Heiner Müller* of *Text + Kritik*, Munich, 1982.

The writers referred to in the interviews are little—if at all—known in the U.S., though they are part of any educated German's intellectual baggage.

Wolfgang Hildesheimer, born in 1916, lived from 1933-46 in England and Palestine; after his return to Germany, he became an acclaimed author of stage and radio plays and the foremost representative of the German variant of theatre of the absurd. Also a novelist, probably his most successful achievement was a brilliant and controversial biography of Mozart.

Ernst Jünger, born in 1895, arguably has become the most influential conservative German writer of his generation. His early works, as *In Thunderstorms of Steel*, described war as man's ultimate existential experience. After a pro-fascist period, he turned his back on German Nazism and attacked it with his metaphoric novel *On the Marble Cliffs*. Of his other prose, *African Games*, *Heliopolis*, *The Boar Hunt*, and *Approaches*, ought to be mentioned.

Paul Celan (1920-1970), is recognized as one of the great German poets of the century.

''Heinz G. Konsalik'' is the pen name of Heinz Günther, born in 1921, an author who had immense commercial success with popular novels about Russia and Eastern Europe, published in illustrated weeklies, hardcover, and numerous paperback editions.

C. W.

A conversation with Uwe Wittstock about constructive fear and the defeatist talk of the world's end, and the writer's task in the nuclear age.

* * *

Is there a desire for an end of the world?

The end of the world has become a faddish problem since it can be accomplished by political means. Earlier, one simply was scientifically aware of the fact that eventually it was going to happen. Since it also can be accomplished by politics, however, it has become a problem that bothers people. Consequently, I consider all the excitement about this topic a bit exaggerated. The end of the world is, first of all, an individual experience. Every normal human being is aware of his/her mortality, and when you die the world ends. That's simply a fact. The bad aspect is that all this talk about the end of the world meanwhile had its effect even in the arts. This end-of-the-world mood and propaganda causes a deterioration or corruption of morale and craft among writers, too. You may know the problem of Wolfgang Hildesheimer—he said in an interview he thinks that writing makes no sense anymore today since mankind will depart from this earth very soon and there won't be ''a posterity artists once, maybe, were able to dream of.'' That is a totally defeatist attitude, I believe. When I'm working on a project, I do so because I like to do this particular work, because I want to do it the best way I can. It's totally irrelevant, after all, if tomorrow the finished product is enshrined in a museum or adrift in the Atlantic, encased in a bottle. I have to do my work as well as I'm able to do it, without considering the consequences or conditions, and also without asking if the material I use will be enduring enough to survive. But currently such defeatism causes a kind of depravation that is pervading all aspects of publishing. There are no standards left. It isn't at all necessary anymore to phrase a sentence carefully enough so, at least, it's grammatically correct. You can scribble down the most revolting kind of shit—it doesn't matter at all, as long as it's selling. And it's being sold with the thought in the back of one's brain: ''Nothing will last very long anyway, at least let's quickly cash in, as long as it lasts.'' That's the main aspect of this talk about the world coming to an end. If it actually does happen, or not, only interests me as a problem of secondary importance.

Do you think there is a desire for annihilation, a joyful anticipation of the apocalypse?

Of course. That's like the situation of the combat soldier which the Germans always wrote best about and also enjoyed most. You're relieved of all responsibilities, of all ties, you're a free man. At some time the order will be given, you'll climb from the trenches and maybe you'll be hit, maybe not. So, you aren't responsible anymore for anything you do. That aspect is the worst of it and such desire, then, is totally negative.

Would you call this a collective death wish?

I wouldn't. It's collective laziness. You're too lazy—I'm remaining within my métièr now—to phrase a sentence the best way you're capable of. You rather look for excuses. That relieves you of any obligation to formulate sentences with precision. It doesn't matter, after all.

In your piece DESCRIPTION OF A PICTURE, you sketch "a land-scape beyond death." What do you imagine the world will be like after the end?

I haven't the foggiest idea; I'd like to know, though. Maybe this isn't a question if you're twenty. I'm fifty-six now and the closer I get to the time of my unavoidable end, the more I'm interested in what death means. I've just read a text by Ernst Jünger who appears to be immortal. He is pondering the idea, or better: it's becoming self-evident to him now that there is a resurrection. I can understand this very well, because Ernst Jünger cannot live without Ernst Jünger. However, I believe you have to be careful that you don't get into a situation where you aren't able to live without yourself anymore; then you will begin to think about the possibility that maybe there is something on the other side, after all. Besides, our understanding of the term "democracy" should imply that we're also thinking about the dead. After all, there are more of the dead than there are of the living—if there is such a thing as "the dead." Consequently, it is democratic to consider the problems of the dead.

Why is today's talk about the end of the world so profitable?

I believe this is a German problem. I even think it is specifically a West German problem. There isn't much money to be made with this topic in the GDR, and there also is a taboo in force that's posited against it. In the Federal Republic there is this noteworthy problem of the birth rate. This may probably sound biological but I do believe there is a connection between spirit-of-life, or attitutde towards life, of a population and its sinking birth rate: a people that wants to die. It wants to relish its life until the end, of course. It doesn't want to give up anything. In this respect, the Federal Republic of Germany is exemplary. Here, they want to drink all the beer themselves, and when they can't drink beer any longer there shouldn't be any beer left.

The images of destruction in your plays mostly are of high aesthetic quality. Do you think the apocalypse is beautiful? Or a provocative question: Is a nuclear mushroom beautiful?

I haven't experienced one. It certainly is a macabre aspect that it can be viewed aesthetically or as an aesthetic event—of course, only by those not afflicted. This is essential. If you're afflicted, the aesthetics are finished. But for those not afflicted, for the observer, it is possible to view it as an aesthetic phenomenon. That certainly has also to do with the utopia which always is invested in apocalyptic imaginations. There is a dammed-up desire for final justice, for a doomsday. On this doomsday, one hopes, at last the wicked will be punished and the good rewarded. This is a deeply internalized human desire. It influences all imaginations of the apocalypse. Some day all bills will be settled, the bottom line will be drawn.

There is also the fear of the end. Can it be overcome by art?

Well, I believe when the fear is gone there is nothing left to stop it. Fear is something immensely pedagogic. Without fear there would be no progress, without fear there would be no culture. And this will remain so in spite of all the inflation of fear that is created by today's media. Such fear also generates creativity. It's constructive. Fear enforces solutions. If you repress fear, you retard resistance against whatever causes fear.

If you want to have political impact with your plays, would you rather have them performed for the UN plenary session or in a training camp for guerillas?

Of course, in the training camp—that's no question. The UN would pay better but the training camp interests me more, since it has more to do with the future than the UN.

Paul Celan wrote: "Death is a master from Germany." In one of your texts you quote Edgar Allan Poe: "The terror I write of isn't from Germany, it is a terror of the soul." You added: "The terror I write of is from Germany." Are the Germans not only especially susceptible to fear of the world's end but also born terrorists?

What do you mean by "born"? In Brecht's notes on *Mother Courage* you'll find the comment: "In the Peasant Wars, the greatest misfortune of German history, the fangs of the Reformation were extracted." I think this emphasis is important. The Peasant Wars were the earliest revolution in Europe and therefore they were the most massively stamped out. This people never recovered from it. Then the Thirty Years' War followed which again trampled down the character of this people. Germany never recovered from that either. Then, in 1848, we had our last chance to fall in step with the rest of Europe. But the middle class revolution was also crushed. Consequently, Germany never closed ranks with Europe. And now the country remains suspended between East and West, and it is always afraid of having no identity. And from fear of having no identity the death wish grows. That is, the desire to destroy or be destroyed. There is something else which comes to my mind in this context: It may sound odd but there is a strange affinity between Germans and Jews. It results from these identity problems. The German isn't "at home," the Jew isn't "at home." The German is alienated from himself, the Jew is alienated from himself, alienated by history. From this affinity, then, came their deadly encounter.

You're dissatisfied that your recent works are only understood in West Germany as plays of disappointment. Which other possible readings do you see?

First of all, there is a basic error: the history of literature or art is always understood and interpreted by the media as a history of contents or an adaptation of contents. The utopian feature can also be the form or the content's expression. That is ignored, I think. The practice of our theatres is concerned with the conveyance of content. Information is conveyed by way of texts, but the text, the form is not conveyed. Plays are only judged by their content: This and that is represented in a play, consequently it is a sad play, and that makes me sad. It isn't at all conveyed that it is a phrased text and that the phrasing of a fact is already a conquest of the fact. The utopian feature is in the form, and not in the content. The form, of course, can only be the last reflex of the possibility of such conquest. It isn't, after all, the conquest itself but merely indicates that the conquest is possible.

You don't think your plays, especially the later ones, are very dark?

Today, there exists a corrupted attitude toward the tragic, or also toward death. In my opinion, an ideal stance would be: "To live without hope and despair." And this has to be learned. I believe, I'm able to. People always ask for hope. That is a Christian question. It wouldn't have been a question for the Greeks, the contemporaries of Socrates: One had neither hope nor despair. One was alive. This attitude toward the tragic as something that enriches life and the theatre has been lost because of Christianity. The tragic is something very vital: I see a man perish and that gives me strength. Nowadays it is the rule, a widely shared response, that it is depressing when someone perishes.

You think, then, your plays are indeed dark but they activate the spectator in spite of it?

I feel activated by a well-phrased line, wherever I read it, whatever it states. Such form is a human achievement, and that is an element of utopia and it gives me strength. People always expect solace from art, always demand that art makes them forget basic facts of their existence. And when art won't provide that, they'll read Konsalik.

Do you nourish hope for something?

I don't need hope. I have enough projects, I have work for years to come, as long as it's possible.

1986